Silver Investing For Beginners

(Invest In REAL MONEY Today For A WEALTHIER FUTURE Tomorrow)

PLUS: Simple Low Cost Way To Get Started

John Roberts

http://www.LiveLearnAndProsper.com/siln

NOTE that for your convenience all web site links referred to in this book are also listed at www.LiveLearnAndProsper.com/si.

SILVER INVESTING FOR BEGINNERS – Invest In REAL MONEY Today For A WEALTHIER FUTURE Tomorrow

Published by Live Learn And Prosper, Orlando, Florida.

Visit us on the web at http://www.LiveLearnAndProsper.com.

Silver Investing For Beginners – 4/28/20 edition - r31 v00

CONTENTS

CONTENTS

1

INTRODUCTION

On January 18, 1980, the price of silver had rocketed upward by 724% in less than a year, from $6 to $50 an ounce. So high in fact, that people formed long lines to cash in their silver at local coin and pawn shops. Ladies were selling their tea sets, families were hocking their silverware and coin collectors were cashing in their collections.

As dramatic as that sounds, leading experts today think silver could dwarf that 1980 event. Some see future increases as high as 5000% or more. They are calling this the opportunity of a lifetime, the greatest wealth transfer in history, from those who don't own silver to those that do.

Yet today, the public is unaware of silver's potential value, and the forces that could propel it to great heights. But after reading this book you'll be ahead of the crowd. You'll know how to turn those forces to your financial advantage and opportunity.

Now, no one knows for sure the future price of silver, not even the experts. So we're not going to shoot for those lofty 5000% profits.

Instead, we're going to talk about a more modest 500% increase over time. That is, if you can consider 500% modest. But at today's price of around $20 an ounce, it's fairly easy to make the case for $100 silver sometime in the future.

And we'll show how silver can also preserve your wealth by protecting you from the ravages of inflation and the devaluation of our currency. And provide financial disaster insurance too.

And you get all of these benefits for free, while poised for a great profit in the future. Which means silver is a great tool to protect your investment portfolio and build a more secure financial future for you and your family.

So are you someone who wants to make money in silver? And does that 1980 silver mania story make you feel excited? Because if you answered yes to those questions, then this book just might be the solution you've been looking for. Because it will show you **just what you need to know to start investing in silver.**

And it will describe all of this for you in simple terms you already understand. Not complicated theory. Not a mind-numbing blitz of technical buzzwords. Just what you need to know and the few specific steps you can take to get started.

So that by the end of this book, you will be able to buy your first ounce of silver. And your first silver stock too, if you wish. **You will know the simple steps to get set for the greatest wealth transfer in history.** And start on your path to a more secure financial future.

How To Use This Book

As you read though this book, you'll see how simple it is to start building your silver investment. And how you are just a few steps away from buying your first ounce of silver. So with that in mind, here's what you'll learn about this exciting investment.

Section 1 is what you are reading now. It's an "Introduction." Let's be realistic here. We won't shoot for lofty 5000% profits that some experts predict. This is just a beginners book. But we can definitely shoot for you increasing and preserving your wealth over time with silver. And positioning yourself for a huge increase should silver explode like it has in the past.

Then in Section 2 we answer the important question, "Why Invest In Silver?" I think you will be surprised at some of the reasons. Some that you may not have thought about. For example, we start off by talking about how our money is literally going broke, and how silver can protect your purchasing power. After all, you work hard for your money. But many investments, like savings accounts and bonds, pay you very little, and lose their value to inflation, year after year.

But silver, over time, can preserve your purchasing power, and even grow your wealth. We'll show you why that is, and how this is one of the best times to get started and invest.

Section 3 is called "Basic Information About Silver." And we really mean basic information here -- just what you need to know to get started. Like the two key measures of silver you invest in - which are weight and purity. And don't worry - we name the simple investments to make, and weight and purity is already baked into them. And we show why we prefer silver over gold. Hint: Believe it or not, the available silver is more scarce than gold. And the prices can rise faster than gold.

Then in Section 4 we get into "The Types Of Silver Investments." And we start with the very simplest one - a special one-ounce silver coin recognized around the world. And you pay just for the silver content, not the coin collecting value. For many people this one type of coin investment is enough. And you don't even need an account to get started. You can go out and buy these coins today.

But there are other interesting types of silver you may wish to invest in. Some of them even pay you quarterly dividends while you own them. And we get into those too.

Section 5 is called "How To Buy Silver." Okay, you'll be surprised how easy this can be. If you are buying physical silver, you can just drive to a special kind of store the same day you read this book. And we'll tell you what to buy and how to ask for it. Or if you're not a brick and mortar store kind of person, there are a number of ways to invest online as well.

I do both, including an automatic purchase and storage program. And I'll show you exactly how I do it and who I do it with.

Then in Section 6 we get into "How Much Silver Should You Own." There's a wide range of opinions on this from the experts. But we narrow that down, and give you three choices, depending on if you are conservative, middle of the road, or a bit aggressive. And we'll tell you the specific percent's of your investable assets that fit these ranges.

And since I put my money were my mouth is, I tell you how much I invest in silver too.

Section 7 is called "Protecting Your Silver Investments." This is mainly about how to safely store your silver or manage your silver investments. And there are a number of options here. And some options you might want to avoid. Hint: You might not want to keep all of your silver in your banks safe deposit box - because there's a big drawback to that. And it could kick in just when you might need your silver the most.

Then we wrap up in the Conclusion Section with "Additional Resources," useful to you as a new silver investor. We cover a number of helpful resources in the book. So this section lists them all for you as a handy reference. And some additional resources are listed as well.

Finally, writing this book has been most gratifying, because I know that many of you can make money with silver investing over time, and protect your investments from the ravages of inflation too.

So I'm excited for you… as you begin building your silver investment in real money today for a wealthier future tomorrow.

So Who Am I And Why Should You Listen To Me?

So who am I and how can I help you with silver investing? Well, I've been involved in silver in one form or another for decades. As you might imagine, there are many ways to invest and speculate in silver, and I've done most of them.

Being fascinated with silver since the early 1980's, I've bought and sold physical silver, including bars, coins, rounds, junk silver and official government bullion coins such as American Silver Eagles and Canadian Maple Leafs.

I've also speculated with silver on margin and traded options on silver futures in the commodity futures market.

By the way, most people don't know that the commodity futures market is 16 times bigger than the stock market. There's a huge amount of money moving through those markets on a daily basis in crude oil, gold, silver, wheat, corn, pork bellies and many more. And yes, I've even speculated in pork bellies too (that's what bacon is made from). And who doesn't love bacon :-).

And in the stock market, I've bought and sold silver mining stocks, silver Exchange Traded Funds (ETF's), and silver streamer stocks. I've personally speculated in options on silver stocks and ETF's as well. And as a former financial consultant and licensed stockbroker, I traded silver options for clients out of my office in Coral Gables, Florida.

Now, if this all sounds complicated, don't worry. Because we're just going to get into the simplest things. They're all you really need to do. And that can save you from making some beginners mistakes like I made when I started.

Because years back, in the 1980's, my first silver investment wasn't so great. I started off buying bags of silver on margin (definitely not recommended as a beginners trade). My trade did well at first, and so I kept adding to my position with my paper profits.

And things were looking just great. But then, of all things, the former Soviet Union anticipated poor grain harvests and dumped millions of dollars in gold on the market to finance grain purchases. And that flood of precious metals hit the silver prices, and this hapless Midwest investor too. Who'd have thought it?

So I watched helplessly as the silver price dropped and I got my first margin call. Which means I had to cough up $1000 within 24 hours, or my position would be sold out at a loss. I covered that first margin call, but then silver dropped again. So I bailed out at a loss as my silver profits dwindled in front of my eyes.

And although the solutions are obvious to me today, I wouldn't have known much what to do back then, even if I'd tried.

Does this story have a familiar sound to you with some of your investments? I was, perhaps, an investor just like you.

Years later I became a financial consultant and licensed stockbroker working for a large broker-dealer in the US. And I also continued to study and invest in silver. And through much research, study, trial and error, I began to understand the answer to my basic question of how to create and preserve wealth with silver.

And if I could do that, starting from such a humble beginning, and making so many mistakes, you can too.

So let's look at how silver investing can increase and protect your wealth. Let's get to the basic question. And that is, "Why invest in silver?"

2

WHY INVEST IN SILVER?

So why bother investing in silver? What's in it for you?

And the answer is that investing in silver can **increase and preserve your wealth** over time when done properly.

And it does this for you in a number of ways.

For example, back in 1964 I could buy a gallon of gasoline for a quarter ($.25) in Springfield, Missouri. Today, many decades of inflation later, gasoline is now at about $3.00 a gallon. But as I stand at the gas pump, filling my tank with that $3.00 gasoline, I find it interesting that you and I can still buy a gallon of gasoline with that same 1964 quarter.

Because that 1964 quarter was made of 90% silver, and that silver is worth $3.00 dollars today. Which means gasoline is still $.25 a gallon in terms of silver quarters.

So you can look at this rather astounding fact a number of ways.

One is that the silver in that quarter has gone up by 1200%, from $.25 to $3.00. So that's definitely **increasing your wealth.**

Another is that it has **preserved your wealth** and purchasing power through all of those years. Because, over fifty years later, you can still buy a gallon of gasoline for the same amount of silver (.18 of an ounce, or about a fifth of an ounce in that quarter). So that silver has protected you from inflation.

And finally, you can see that the dollar has seriously dropped in value over the years. Because a gallon of gasoline used to only cost a fourth of a dollar (twenty-five cents). Now it costs three whole dollars. That's a 92% loss of value.

So let's not mince words here. That's a serious loss of purchasing power and devaluation of currency. Our currency is literally going broke. Our dollars have clearly dropped in value. By quite a lot, actually.

But not silver. Silver hasn't dropped in value at all in this example. So silver, as money, has given you a profit, financial security and clearly stood the test of time.

But the dollar (and other paper currencies) have not. We know that because we see inflation in the prices of all of the things we buy with our dollars. Year by year, little by little, our paper currency has been debased and diluted, and literally been going broke in front of our eyes.

So how did we get this way? What's going on here? And what's causing this?

INVESTING, SPECULATING AND HEDGING: Note that while I often use the term silver "investing," technically, much of what we're talking about is not investing, but rather speculating. I just use the term investing loosely because it's generally understood. And for many readers, the distinction probably doesn't make much difference. You're buying silver in one form or another to achieve a financial goal.

But for those who want to put a fine point on it, **speculating** is when you buy something thinking that the price will go up in the future. Then you will sell it at that higher price and pocket the difference as a profit.

For example, let's say you're buying silver at $20 ounce today. And you're hoping it will jump to $50 an ounce in the future, like it did in 1980, or 2011. If this hap-pens, you plan to sell your silver, and pocket the $30 price difference as your profit. If that is your plan, then you are speculating.

Investing is when you buy something that will pay you money - like a dividend paying stock or a business. So if you buy a silver mining stock that pays you dividends, then you truly are "investing" in silver.

Interestingly, the value of the mine and the stock may go up in price as well, so you may also get the benefits of speculating with the stock.

And then there is **hedging**, which is when you buy something that will protect you by going up when your other investments go down. For example, when the stock market drops, many people get worried and start buying precious metals such as gold and silver for safety.

This can cause the precious metals price to go up, and make up for the drop in their stock investments. So the precious metals they have in their portfolio help protect them from other losses.

Similarly, silver might protect you if there was ever a serious financial disaster. For example, if the banking system locked up, and none of the ATM's worked, and you couldn't get access to your bank account, then having some physical silver would allow you to still buy food and other necessities for you and your loved ones. So that's another hedging example of protecting yourself from an adverse event.

Interestingly, if you buy silver bullion and also invest in some of the dividend paying stocks in this book, you're doing all three things at once with silver. You're speculating, investing and hedging.

The Problem: Our Currency Is Going Broke

Well, it turns out that governments are the cause of all of this currency debasement and inflation. They've done this for thousands of years, and the story is ALWAYS the same.

It goes something like this. In the beginning, a country creates money so their citizens can buy goods, do business, save, and of course, pay their taxes. And typically that money is in the form of coins made of precious metals like silver or gold. It's good, honest money and the citizens know they can count on it.

And prices are pretty stable too. I mean, if a gallon of milk costs one silver coin, ten years later, it still costs about one silver coin. Ditto for savings. If people hide away a thousand silver coins under their mattress for a rainy day, then ten years later, if they take them out to spend, they're still worth about the same. They've not lost value.

Of course, lugging around a thousand silver coins (about 60 pounds at one ounce each) is kind of inconvenient. So the government creates paper currency too. Let's call this paper currency dollars, with each paper dollar worth one silver coin.

SILVER AND DOLLARS: The word dollar is of German origin from the beginning of the 16th century. It was named after a town called Joachimsthal, or Joachims Thal, which meant Joachim's Valley.

Why was this town so important? Because it had a silver mine, and they began to produce silver coins of uniform weight and fineness. These coins were of such quality they came into good repute all over Europe and were called Joachim's thalers.

Over time they just started calling the silver coins "thalers". Thaler eventually changed to daler, and finally dollar.

The term was later applied to a coin used in the Spanish-American colonies. It was widely used in the British North American colonies at the time of the American War of Independence, and was adopted as the name of the US monetary unit in the late 18th century.

The government makes sure that for each dollar they print, they have a silver coin in the banking system to back it up. So if you want to, you can just go to the bank and give them a paper dollar, and they'll give you a silver coin. Or you can give them a silver coin and they'll give you a dollar.

It's all the same, really. The paper dollar is just a claim check on one silver coin.

So now you don't have to lug around all of your silver coins any more. You just carry your paper dollars and buy things with them. And everyone accepts them instead of silver coins, because they know they can just go to the bank and get the silver coins any time they want.

And the government accepts these paper silver dollars too, when you pay your taxes. And the government only spends as many dollars each year as they get in taxes. And they are always careful to only print as many paper dollars as they have silver coins in the banking system.

So everyone is confident in the money system. It's good, sound money. And things go along just great for a while.

But then, some of the country's politicians get worried about winning their next election. And so they start promising benefits to the citizens, that the country can't afford, in order to get re-elected. In other words, they're promising benefits that cost more than the taxes they are going to receive. They are creating debt - a national debt.

Essentially, they're trying to buy votes, with your money, to stay in power. And if enough citizens are good with that, because hey, who can say no to "free" benefits, then they get re-elected and stay in power.

Panem Et Circenses (Bread and Circuses): There's actually a phrase for these free benefits called "bread and circuses." And you may hear it from time to time today. I heard "bread and circuses" mentioned on the news just the other day.

It captures a certain cynical view that the masses can be kept happy with free benefits and diversions provided by the government.

It was first used around A.D. 100 by a Roman poet who was poking fun at the populace. He deplored how shallow and unheroic the Roman citizens had become after the Roman Republic ceased to exist and the Roman Empire began.

He said, "Two things only the people anxiously desire — **bread and circuses.**"

The government at that time kept the Roman populace happy by distributing free food and staging huge spectacles at the coliseum. Meanwhile, they were stealing from the citizens by devaluing their currency, and getting away with murder (literally).

And along the way, these politicians also get the country involved in some expensive wars that the country can't afford either. These wars may be for legitimate defense reasons, or ideological reasons, or because some of their big campaign contributors make money from the wars, or for some other reason.

The reason doesn't really matter. Because the bottom line is that now the government has created even more debt than it can pay with the taxes it receives.

So some of the politicians propose raising taxes to pay that debt. But this idea is not so popular with the citizens, and so those politicians don't get re-elected.

Other politicians, seeing the fate of their peers, think of another way to pay the bills. They tell the Treasury to just print more paper dollars, even though they don't have enough silver coins to back them up. And then they pay the government's bills with these new, watered down, diluted dollars.

This looks like it solves the problem because all of the bills get paid and they don't have to raise taxes. And they can keep giving out these "free" benefits and get re-elected.

But of course this doesn't really solve the problem. Because those new paper dollars are not backed by silver. So ALL of the dollars in the country become worth less than before.

Here's why. Let's say that in the beginning the country was very small and the government had a million silver coins in the banking system. And they printed a million dollar bills. So a dollar bill was worth one silver coin. Okay, good so far. That's good, sound money.

But then the government created another million dollars in debt, and printed another million paper dollars to pay it. So now there are two million paper dollars in circulation. But there are still only one million silver coins in the banks. So now a paper dollar is only worth half of a silver coin. It has lost a lot of value.

That's kind of a big deal. Because now, if you had saved a thousand paper dollars and kept them under your mattress, or in your savings account, your savings have lost 50% of their value. Your savings, which used to be worth 1000 silver coins, are now only worth 500 silver coins. You just lost half of your savings.

And as you will see, that's what's going on today. The government keeps spending more and more that it can't pay for. So it keeps printing more and more new currency out of thin air. And the banking system is flooded with more and more dollars that are worth less and less.

Actually, the situation is even worse, because the government, through the Federal Reserve, doesn't even need to bother with printing all of those pesky paper dollars. In our computerized age, they can just create electronic deposits. This is essentially the same as printing dollars, but happens with no printing cost at all, at the click of a mouse. And the banking system is flooded with even more, less valuable, electronic dollars.

And so your savings, wealth and purchasing power are getting destroyed, year by year. And prices keep going up, because the dollars are worth less and less.

That's called inflation, and it's why you feel like you just can't get ahead.

But this is not a new thing. Like I said earlier, governments have been doing this for thousands of years, even before there were paper and electronic currencies.

So how did they do this? To find out, let's go back in time to the sad story of Silvus Ruinous. Because I think his story is going to have a familiar ring to you.

$833 Cup Of Coffee - Now That's Inflation! Inflation and price increases can go to incredible levels. And it's happening right now in Venezuela. While the US currently has averaged an inflation rate of around 3% per year, as of this writing Venezuela has a rate of over 43,000% per year - and rising.

Okay, so that's a big number, but what does it really mean? Well, in 2016 a cup of coffee costs around 450 Venezuelan Bolivars. And as I write this book, just two years later, that same cup of coffee costs 1,000,000 Bolivars. Since the average Venezuelan wage is $5,000,000 Bolivars per month, it takes a full month's wages to buy just five cups of coffee.

So how much would a cup of coffee cost in the US if five cups cost a month's wages? Well, if we say the average monthly wage is $4166 ($50,000 per year / 12) then five cups of coffee would be $4166.

The Sad Story Of Silvus Ruinus

Figure 2-1. Ancient Roman Silver Coin

So we've seen how modern governments devalue their currencies and cause inflation. It's easy. They just create more of their currency. Like here in the US, where they just print more dollars, or create electronic dollars out of thin air with the click of a mouse.

But how did the ancients do that before paper and electronic currencies were invented? How did they devalue real silver coins?

Well, let's imagine an emperor 2000 years ago named Silvus Ruinus. And Silvus ordered the treasury to create pure one ounce silver coins with his face stamped on them. Okay, so there may have been a bit of ego going on there, but it was good, honest money. And the people knew they could count on its value.

But Silvus was always worried about staying in power. After all, it was good to be the emperor. So, not wanting the people to revolt, he promised them free bread. And free circuses too, down at the colosseum, with lions and gladiators, to keep them entertained. And Silvus became quite popular.

But the free bread and circuses were expensive and this was causing a problem. After all, Silvus had to pay the bread merchants. And the circus operators too, for their expensive lions and gladiators performing down at the colosseum (which was all the rage way back then before cable TV).

And when it came time to pay the bills, and he counted the taxes he'd collected, he only had half as many silver coins in the treasury as he needed to pay the bills. So he started a war with another country to steal their silver mines. But the war didn't go so well, and the cost of the soldiers was even more expensive.

So things were looking pretty bad for his future. Because if he didn't keep providing free bread and circuses, his citizens were going to revolt. And worse yet, what would happen if he didn't pay his soldiers?

So, what did our beleaguered emperor Silvus do?

It's simple, really. He just told the treasury to remake the coins out of equal parts of pure silver and cheap lead. That would double his coins and he could pay the bills. And he could keep giving out free bread and circuses, and pay his soldiers. And keep his job (and life) as emperor, because the people and the soldiers wouldn't revolt.

So the Treasury made all of the new, cheap, silver and lead coins. And they looked just like the original pure silver coins. And the unsuspecting merchants and soldiers all got paid with these devalued coins. So his subjects continued to get their free bread and circuses, and the soldiers fought on.

Problem solved, and things looked good again.

But soon, the merchants caught on to the fact that the coins are just half silver. So they doubled their prices, so they'd still get paid the same amount of silver as before. They started charging two coins for a big loaf of bread. And the lions and gladiators for the colosseum... well, they used to go for 100 coins each, but now they cost 200 coins. And the soldiers demanded that their wages double too.

And there you have it. Welcome to the first inflation in history. Because now all of the prices in the empire had doubled.

And the new, devalued coins didn't just affect the prices of bread and circuses. The prices of togas, sandals, meat, gruel, vegetables, hovels and houses, horses and wagons, and all of the other necessities of life skyrocketed as well.

There was some serious, 100% price inflation going on in the empire. And it was all created by Silvus, the "government."

So all of his subjects, and soldiers too, began getting pretty restless.

And the situation got even worse. Because the next time the bills came due, the Treasury told Silvus that since all of the prices had doubled, well, yet again, he didn't have enough coins to pay the bills. As a matter of fact, he only had half of the silver / lead coins he needed to pay for everything.

So what did Silvus do? Well, he told the treasury to add even 50% MORE lead to the silver / lead coins. That would double his coins again, and he could pay all of his bills (although now the coins would be made of 75% cheap lead and only 25% silver).

So, problem solved again. But you can see where this is going.

Because the situation just kept getting worse, with his subjects catching on to the coins being devalued more and more over time. And prices just kept going higher and higher, as Silvus continued to dilute his coins with more and more cheap lead. Until one day, the coins were pretty much just worthless lead coins with a slight trace of silver in them.

So the vendors stopped making free bread for the people, and there were no more new lions and gladiators brought down to the colosseum. And the people were hungry and bored, and the soldiers angrily started marching home in revolt.

And they threw Silvus into the colosseum with a couple of mangy, old lions left over from last week's circus, which resulted in an unpleasant and final end to his government career.

And there was much turmoil in the empire.

Then a new ruler named Newro came into power and, noticing the fate of his predecessor Silvus Ruinus, promised to mint honest money again. So he had the treasury start making pure silver coins. And he decreed that he would exchange one new silver coin for 50 of the old lead coins.

So there was good, honest money in the empire again.

But all of the people who'd saved money with the old lead coins lost all of their savings at that exchange rate. Because their old coins were basically worthless lead coins with just a trace of silver in them. So they didn't get many new silver coins when they traded their old coins in.

And they had to sell their hovels and houses for next to nothing, because they didn't have enough new silver coins to make their house payments.

But there were a few smart subjects in the empire who had kept, or invested in, the old, original pure silver coins. And so, with pure silver coins, new or old, now 50 times greater in value than the old lead / silver coins, the value of their wealth in coins exploded 5000% overnight!

And so they bought up all of the hovels and houses. And there was a great transfer of wealth in the land, from those who did not have real silver coins, now homeless, to those who did. So many people were still unhappy and restless.

And so Newro, who was really enjoying being the emperor, started to worry about staying in power too. So he also began giving out free bread. And he restarted the circuses at the colosseum as a diversion to keep his subjects from revolting.

Of course, just like Silvus, he couldn't afford all of this. But thinking he could be much more clever than Silvus, he very slowly, very gradually, started putting lead into the new silver coins as well.

But you know how this story is going to end, right? Newro is going to have a bad end to his government career as well.

So why would he do this?

To pay the bills of course. **And because throughout history, rulers and governments just can't resist the temptation to overspend to stay in power.** So they steal money from their citizens by devaluing the currency. Rinse and repeat… history is littered with this same story, again and again.

So okay, fanciful little stories of ancient emperors aside, where do we stand in modern times? And how does this affect you, and your purchasing power and investing in silver today?

The Dollar And Silver Today

You would think that governments and citizens would learn a lesson from thousands of years of currency devaluation and bad endings. But that's not the case. Sadly, our modern situation seems headed in the same downward direction.

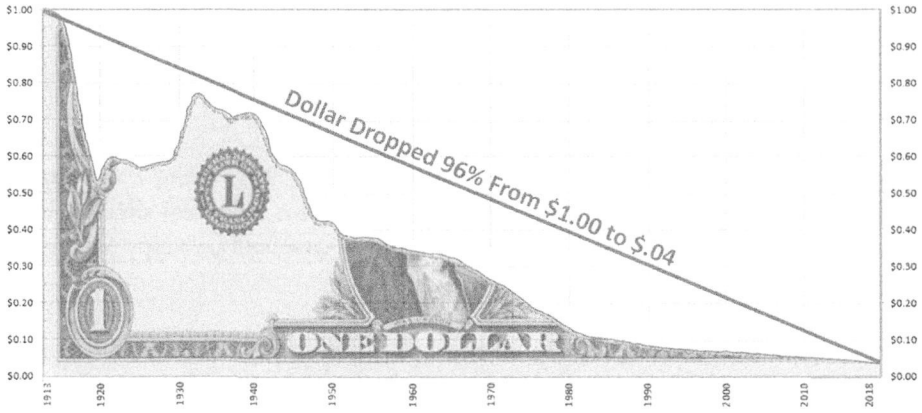

Figure 2-2. 1913 To 2018 - The Dollar Today Is Only Worth 4 Cents

This is apparent when we look at the dollar in the modern era from 1913 to today. The dollar has lost 96% of its value since 1913. So a dollar today is only worth 4 cents of what it was worth in 1913. That's a pretty serious decline in purchasing power.

And as more government debt is created by overspending, more dollars are printed or electronically created. So they continue to lose even more value.

You can see how fast our debt is increasing by looking at the US National Debt Clock here - http://www.usdebtclock.org/. Be sure and look it up. Because it's staggering how fast our debt is increasing right in front of your eyes. For example, in the five minutes it takes you to read this chapter, our debt increased by about $10,000,000 dollars.

But what about silver over the same time period? Well, unlike the dollar, which has declined in value, silver has gone up. By quite a bit, actually. The price of silver looks like this.

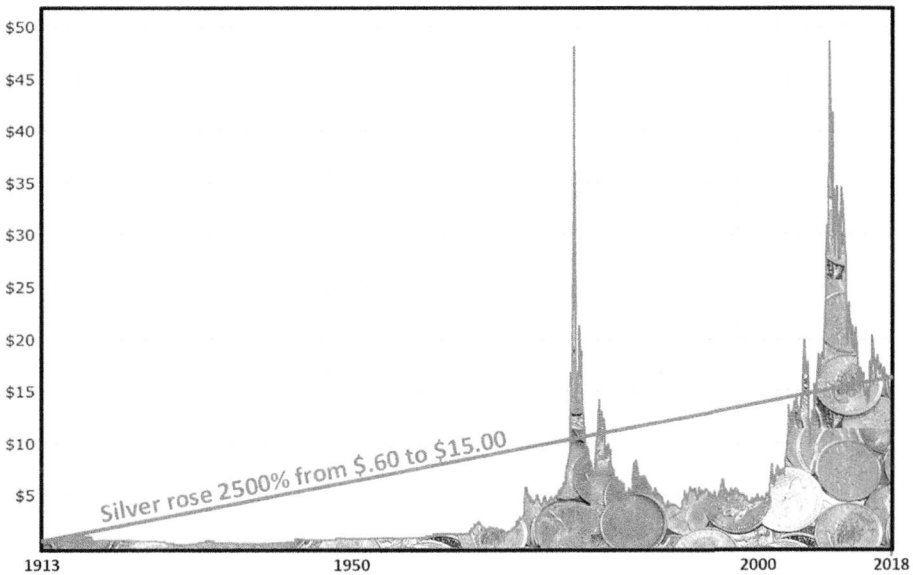

$50
$45
$40
$35
$30
$25
$20
$15
$10
$5

Silver rose 2500% from $.60 to $15.00

1913   1950   2000   2018

Figure 2-3. 21913 To 2018 - Silver Has Gone Up 2500%

Silver has gone up from 60 cents an ounce in 1913 to $15.00 per ounce in 2018. That's a whopping 2500% increase in value ($.60 X 2500% = $15.00).

So if someone (a really long-lived person) had put 1000 dollar bills under their mattress in 1913, then in 2018 that $1000 would only be worth $40. But they could have bought 1667 ounces of silver back in 1913 at $.60 per ounce with their $1000. And if they had done that instead, their $1000 of silver would be worth over $25,000 in 2018.

So, $40 or $25,000. Which would you rather have today?

Let's put the two charts together and ask the same question. Just looking at the increase in silver and the decrease in the dollar (in percents), which is the better place to put your money?

And the answer is silver, of course.

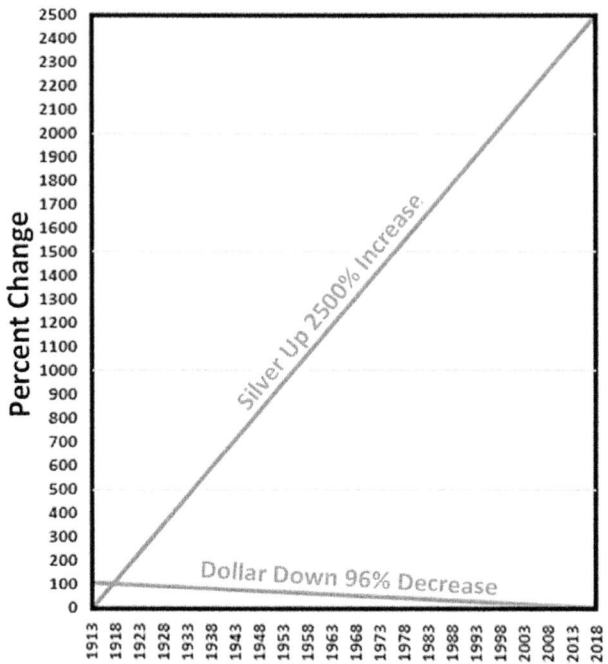

Figure 2-4. 1913 To 2018 - The Dollar And Silver - Where Would You Like Your Money To Be?

Now as a smart reader you might say, well, yes, but that $25,000 today is only worth 4 cents on the dollar of 1913 dollars. And that's another way to look at it. That $25,000 today would be worth $1000 1913 dollars (.04 x $25,000 = $1000).

But that's actually good news, and the point of this exercise. Because you can say their money, through all of those years, had not lost value.

Which is one of main reasons we invest in silver and other precious metals - to preserve our wealth and purchasing power over time.

Okay, so preserving purchasing power is great, but how about making money? Well, this is where it gets really interesting. Because the silver price could explode sometime in the future.

Car Prices In Silver: Let's cross-check those prices. So in 1913, you could buy a new Model T Ford for about $500, or a Chevy for $1500 or more, depending on the model. So a rough average of the car price back then could be around $1000 (or 1667 ounces of silver at $.60 an ounce).

And today, over 100 years later, you can still buy a new car for 1667 ounces of silver. With silver at around $15 an ounce today, that's $25,000. Now that's preserving purchasing power!

You Could Make A Lot Of Money

As we've said earlier, leading experts today think future silver prices could eventually increase as high as 5000%, and they are calling this the opportunity of a lifetime.

And while it's more reasonable to shoot for a more modest 500% over time, 5000% is not as outlandish as it may sound. For example, many people don't realize this, but silver rose 3,646% in the 1970s, from its November '71 low to its January 1980 high. So there's already an historical precedent for huge price increases.

But today the general public is unaware of silver's value, and the forces that could propel it to great heights. Some entertaining and revealing street interviews of people in Southern California clearly show this.

The Public Is Unaware Of Silver's Value

The interviews were conducted by Mark Shouldice (Mark Dice), an internet personality. In the interviews, he approached people on the street by telling them, "Congratulations, you've won a 10-ounce bar of silver or a chilled king-sized Hershey chocolate bar. Which one do you prefer?"

All ten people chose the chocolate bar, worth $1.50!

None of them chose the silver bar, more than half a pound of silver, worth over $150. In other words, they could have bought 100 chocolate bars with the 10 oz silver bar.

But no one understood the value of the silver bar or what they could do with it. As one interviewee said, "I don't have any way to do anything with the silver."

So he took the chocolate bar, even though Mark had deliberately conducted the interviews right in front of a coin shop, where he could have easily checked out the price of the silver bar. Or better yet, taken his free silver bar and cashed it in on the spot.

Eventually, in a not so subtle hint, Mark even suggested to an interviewee that they could step into the coin shop to verify the authenticity of the silver bar. No doubt this would have led to discovering it's $150 value. But instead he was told, "I always take chocolate."

You can see these surprising interviews on YouTube at Chocolate or Silver Street Interviews. Or just Google search on "Mark Dice silver or chocolate bar."

So the public is currently blind to the value of silver, and its potential as an investment.

Perhaps this is not so surprising. After all, the last generation to live under a silver and gold currency standard are the baby boomers. Back then, a paper dollar bill could be exchanged for real silver. Dollar bills actually said "Silver Certificate" on them. And the coins were made of 90% silver too.

So the government would only print as many paper dollar bills (more or less) than they had silver and gold to back them up. It was real money back then, with real value.

Today that limit is gone and they just print money out of thin air. Our coins no longer contain silver, and our dollar bills no longer say Silver Certificate. Instead they just say Federal Reserve Note, which is currency backed by nothing but a bunch of IOU's from the government.

And so, all generations since the boomers have lived under a paper currency situation not backed by silver.

Virtually No One Is Investing In Silver

Not understanding the value of silver means people don't invest in it either. This is borne out by investment newsletters and consultants that advise people to buy precious metals. They estimate that only 2% of the American population own precious metals of any kind – excluding jewelry, of course.

So the public's lack of awareness means you can buy silver at very undervalued prices today. And that leads to an opportunity. Because the best time to get into an investment is before the general public becomes aware of it.

NOT EVEN THE TEA PARTY INVESTED: According to a detailed 2010 poll, only 5% of Tea Party sympathizers were investing in precious metals. Which is surprising, since they supported the return to a gold standard and a gold-backed dollar back then. But only 5% said they had purchased gold coins or bars in the preceding 12 months.

Just imagine what happens to the silver price when the other 98% of the public wake up and rush out to buy it. Silver will be in all of the news reports and headlines of the day. And there will be a mad rush to buy it.

The Silver Price Could Go To The Moon

Just doing the math here, if 2% are buying now, and that jumps to 100% of the population buying, that's 50 times more people, or a 5000% increase in demand.

There's that 5000% number again, isn't it.

The price will skyrocket. And of course, in these manias, like the one we described in 1980, the price could overshoot the value and go even higher.

Realistically, of course, not everyone will pile in and buy silver. But it's safe to say that many people will rush to buy silver if and when the mania happens.

Okay, manias and lack of public awareness aside, there are other reasons silver is poised to soar in the future. And industrial consumption is a big one.

Silver is used in batteries, dentistry, glass coatings, LED chips, medicine, nuclear reactors, solar energy, RFID chips for tracking parcels in shipment, semiconductors, touch screens, water purification, wood preservatives and many other industrial uses. Called the indispensable metal, industrial uses account for at least 50% of the world's consumption.

And consumption is going up. For example, just think of the rise of solar panel usage in recent years to generate climate friendly electrical power.

But here's the thing. The supply of silver is not keeping up. And the supply of scrap silver coming onto the market is actually falling off.

That's a supply and demand problem. So when supply is not keeping up with a growing demand, the price will ultimately rise. This thought is supported by David Morgan, a leading expert in silver and author of *The Silver Manifesto*. He says, "At some point in the next 5 years the price of silver is destined to reach triple-digit prices, or over 6 times greater than the present (~$17-$18 as of this writing). With silver, the potential is exceptionally strong because of required industrial consumption, which will greatly augment the coming effects of significantly higher investment or monetary demand...".

Another reason there will be a shortage of silver is the small size of the silver market. While there is estimated to be 17 times as much silver in the earth as gold, the above ground supply of silver is 5-7 times LESS than gold. A market that small and tight can only go up in the future as shortages appear.

And there's yet another, darker reason that silver could soar. And that is sus-pected big manipulators in the silver market, who may be holding the price down. And while they may be getting away with the manipulation now, they could eventually have to buy a lot of silver to cover their positions. So we'll cover that fascinating reason in a minute.

But suffice to say that the forces are lining up to propel the silver price much higher.

Of course, no one knows when this will happen. It could happen tomorrow, next month or 5-10 years from now. But with historical precedents, the cur-rent lack of investment interest, industrial shortfalls and possible market ma-nipulation, a price rise seems likely over time.

And all of these factors combined with today's low price present a great op-portunity. Because silver investing is cheaper than ever before.

Silver Is Affordable

So affordability is another great advantage of silver as a precious metals invest-ment. At a price of around $15 - $20 an ounce, silver is affordable to most people. That's unlike gold, the other main precious metal, which is around $1300 an ounce.

With the median income in the United States of around $56,000 a year, most people just don't have $1300 laying around to buy an ounce of gold for their precious metals investments.

True, you can buy 1/2 ounce or 1/4 ounce gold coins. And even 1/10 ounce (I own some of the 1/10 ounce gold South African Krugerrands).

But even 1/10th of an ounce is still $130 to shell out. And many people have tight budgets, and that would put quite a strain on them to buy and invest in even these small fractional coins on a regular basis.

For example, according to a recent Federal Reserve Board report, 40% of Americans can't cover a $400 emergency expense. Those who don't have the cash on hand say they'd have to cover it by borrowing or selling something.

But they may have $20 to buy an ounce of silver from time to time. Or if that's too steep, I even discuss later on where you can start for just $3.

Speaking of affordability, I recall a visit to my local coin dealer. I had to wait as he worked with a couple of teenagers. After they left, he told me they mowed lawns, and always brought their lawn mowing money in to buy silver coins.

I was impressed that they had so much investment foresight. Talk about wisdom from the mouths of babes. But this also clearly illustrates silver's investment affordability. Because if teenagers can do it with their lawn mowing money, most adults can too.

This is why silver is often called the poor man's gold. Because compared to gold, just about anyone can afford to start slowly accumulating a precious metals investment in the form of silver.

So all that said, it's clear that silver is very affordable. And this is another big advantage of it as a precious metals investment for most people.

Silver Investing Is Historically Cheap

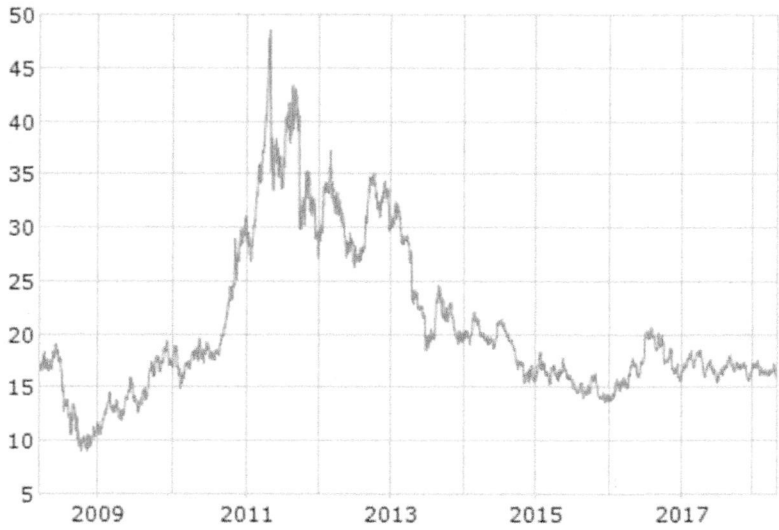

Figure 2-5. Historical Silver Price Chart (US Dollars per Ounce)

We've all heard the old investing adage to buy low and sell high. Buying any investment for an extremely low price is where the real serious money is made. The same goes for buying and investing in silver. And the chart above shows that the price of silver is indeed at the low end over ten years.

And there's another revealing way to measure silver's historical price. And that is to compare its price to the price of gold. So let's just do that now.

At writing today, an ounce of gold will buy you 80 ounces of silver. Wow, that's a lot of silver for just one ounce of gold. Which means silver is really cheap, to get that many ounces for just one ounce of gold.

But on average over the last century, silver has been much more valuable. So much so that one ounce of gold would only buy you 40 ounces of silver. So using that measure, the price of silver is almost 50% lower than that average.

But it gets even better. Because, using the historic average of silver, one ounce of gold would only buy you about 16 ounces of silver.

Here's a new term for you: the gold-to-silver ratio. You will run into this often when investing in silver. It's stated as the amount of silver it takes to purchase one ounce of gold.

So in the example above, it would take 80 ounces of silver to buy 1 ounce of gold. Or put another way, you could buy 80 ounces of silver with 1 ounce of gold. So the gold to silver ratio in this example would be 80 to 1, or 80:1.

That means silver is selling for an 80% discount to its historic price!

Just think about that. Visualize going shopping in one of the major department stores like Macy's or Selfridges. And as you walk into the store, you see a sign that says Levi's and shoes are on sale for 80% off.

That would get your attention, right. Because that's one heck of a sales discount. So silver is clearly on sale today. So it's a good setup for the buy low, sell high scenario.

Is 16:1 really credible or not? Well, here's another factoid for you. According to geological studies, there's 17.5 times as much silver as gold in the earth's crust.

On its own, this suggests the gold price should be about 17.5 times that of silver. That's close enough for me. I'd say that makes the 16:1 gold to silver ratio pretty credible, wouldn't you.

And while we're at it, here's another thing about buying low and selling high. And that is that typically, the lower you buy an investment, the lower your risk.

That's because if the price is already low, the odds of it moving down more are lower.

So while silver can be pretty volatile, it's historically priced so low that the risk of buying it is much lower than in the past. So that's another reason to invest in silver.

But if silver is so valuable, and a good investment, why is it so cheap? What's going on here?

Well, as we showed earlier, the public is generally unaware of the value of silver. So they aren't creating much demand for it - yet. But as I alluded to earlier, there may be another, hidden factor as well. And you aren't going to believe this.

Why Is Silver So Cheap?

A number of credible experts believe the silver market is being manipulated to keep the price down. And the names of the same big banks keep coming up in this regard.

For example, Deutsche Bank was fined $38 million to settle a silver market rigging lawsuit in 2016. And during that investigation, a number of other banks and holding companies were implicated as well.

Now, normally I run away from any investment that shows accounting or price irregularities. For example, if I hear of accounting problems in a stock I own, I get rid of it. Or if I'm thinking about buying it - I don't.

Because it's hard enough to invest well without a bunch of funny business going on. Like the Enron scandal in the past, where management deliberately falsified their revenues, quarter after quarter, until someone caught on. Then the price plummeted from $90 a share to virtually zero ($.61) and wiped out the investors.

But in the case of silver, I'm a long term buyer. So if some banks are going to bend the rules to keep the price down, I'll just keep buying. Because their actions are subsidizing my purchases of silver by depressing the price. They're helping me buy at a discount.

You may wonder how they can do this - how they can manipulate the silver market. And the short answer is that some of their traders may be selling large amounts of silver that they don't own, and that doesn't exist, i.e. fake silver. That floods the market with silver sales transactions, and fools it into thinking there's a big surplus. And so the price goes down.

But eventually, their actions are going to catch up with them. Because instead of a surplus, the silver supply will probably continue to tighten. And at some critical point in the future, some big player is going to ask to take delivery of real silver.

A number of experts believe it's only a matter of time before this perfect storm happens. And then the jig is up for the traders with the fake silver. Because they will need to buy a lot of real, physical silver to cover their paper silver obligations.

And like we said earlier, when a lot of silver, or anything for that matter, is being bought, the price goes up. In this case, it will probably go up dramatically because of the huge amounts involved. So this is a great reason to buy silver now, before the demand and price spike.

And speaking of huge demand and dramatic price increases, that takes us straight to our final reason to own silver. And that is that owning silver gives you a form of financial and natural disaster insurance.

I really hope we never have to use it for that reason, but the subject needs exploring. Because disasters do happen. And they can affect your money and ability to buy necessities. We've had a number of warnings of this over the past decades.

In fact, one of those warnings happened to me on Tuesday morning, October 25, 2005. And it definitely affected my money and ability to buy necessities. To learn more, read on.

EXTRA CREDIT: How The Silver Market May Be Manipulated. It looks like at least four major traders use the New York Commodities and Mercantile Exchange to sell large amounts of silver.

Remember, when a lot of silver, or anything for that matter, is being bought, the price usually goes up. But when a lot of silver is being sold, the price typically goes down.

Now there's nothing wrong with someone selling a lot of silver. If you own a lot of silver and want to sell it, no problem. It's yours to do with what you like.

But some of the big players are selling it on the futures market. They aren't selling physical silver. They're selling futures contracts, which are just a promise that they will provide the buyer with a certain amount of silver, at a certain price, at a future date. And they probably don't even own the silver they are selling.

Now there's nothing particularly wrong with selling futures contracts and things you don't own. Farmers do it all of the time. They may sell futures on their crops before they are even harvested, or planted, for that matter. This just means they promise to deliver a certain amount of grain from their acreage at a certain price, at a future date. This allows the farmers to know what their price, and profit, will be in advance, and lock it in.

But a prudent, honest farmer will typically only sell as many futures contracts of grain as his acreage can produce.

But not so with some silver traders. There's evidence that they collectively sell double the amount of silver known to exist on the planet! In other words, they are selling silver that doesn't even exist, and never will.

It's fake silver. So these huge artificial selling positions fool the market into thinking that twice as much silver is coming on to the market in the future. And so the price goes artificially down. Because the market thinks there is a glut of silver, when in fact there is not.

To put that in perspective, of all the commodities out there (gold, oil, wheat, cattle, etc.), none have such a huge short position as silver. For example, only 2% of gold that exists is sold in futures contracts. But the silver traders are selling 200% of the silver commodity.

That smacks of some real funny business going on.

But eventually, as the available silver gets more scarce, and the demand keeps increasing, they will not be able to hold the price down. Because they will have to deliver on their contracts.

And since they don't own all of the silver they have sold, they'll have to go into the market and buy huge amounts to cover their positions. And this could cause the price to explode.

Silver Gives You Disaster Insurance

Figure 2-6. Hurricane Wilma
Image source www.Wikipedia.com

On Tuesday morning, October 25, 2005, I found myself standing in line outside the darkened doorway of a Radio Shack store just north of Ft. Lauderdale. I wanted to buy some extra radio batteries, but this was no ordinary purchase.

The people in the long line behind me talked in hushed tones, and it was eerily quiet throughout the entire shopping center. Even though it was 10:00 in the morning, there was absolutely no traffic in this normally busy shopping center.

The parking lot was virtually empty, except for tree limbs, and entire palm trees, which were blown down and scattered all over the place. And I had been forced to drive off the road a number of times to get here, to bypass huge uprooted trees.

As I stood in line, my mind flashed back to the howling wind the night before. And how as I watched from my eighth floor condo balcony, a terrific gust had suddenly swirled about me, and low pressure started to lift me up, trying to throw me over the balcony. So I had beat feet into a nearby concrete stairwell, away from any glass, and ridden out the storm inside.

My attention snapped back to the present, and the store owner at the door, who was only letting one person into his shop at a time. It was my turn.

And I was glad I had cash, because he was only doing business with cash customers. That's because the power was out, and electronic cash registers, credit cards and ATM's were not working. And I mean really not working anywhere - for miles and miles.

This surreal scene was of the catastrophic effects of Hurricane Wilma I had just survived the day before. Wilma turned out to be the second-costliest Florida hurricane ever recorded, killing 26 people, and leaving 6,000,000 people without power. Considered a freakish storm, it was the worst hurricane to hit Ft. Lauderdale in 50 years.

Little did I know at the time that 20 days later many residents and businesses, myself included, would still not have power. Which meant the elevator to my eighth floor condo was out and required lugging bags of ice and more supplies up 16 flights of stairs. And cable TV, internet, cell phone services, ATM's and credit card purchases would be unavailable for up to two months in some areas.

Walking into the dark store, barely lit by daylight from the front door, I searched and found the batteries I wanted, handed the owner cash, and left as he motioned to the next person in line.

And I heard him ask, "Do you have cash?" Because if they didn't, they were out of luck, no matter how great their need. Because this natural disaster had affected everything, including the electronic financial system we all take for granted. Debit and credit cards were worthless, requiring all to use cash.

But as bad as it was, it was still just a local South Florida problem.

But what about a national disaster? When even the soundness of the government and financial system is threatened? What if confidence in our money was lost? Because we know that our money is going broke with all of our deficit spending, debt and inflation.

We've gotten some warnings and near misses on this. For example, the US came within hours of a financial crisis, during the crash of 2008-2009. Overspending, bad loans and too much credit virtually locked the system up, and a disaster was narrowly averted. And the Great Recession followed.

And then, as recently as 2010 - 2011, there was immense risk to the national and world economy. As the 2010 U.S. midterm elections loomed, there was a deficit reduction battle between President Obama and the Tea Party. So much so that the silver price rose steadily from $17 to $25-$30, settling in at about $25.

Then in 2011 the United States debt ceiling crisis hit. And on April 18, 2011, U.S.-based rating agency Standard & Poor's issued a shocking "negative" outlook on the U.S.'s "AAA" credit rating for the first time since the rating agency began in 1860. They gave a 1 in 3 chance that it would be reduced over the next two years.

In other words, the unthinkable seemed about to happen. The US bonds, thought to be the safest in the world, were about to be downgraded due to the threat of the federal government not paying its obligations. Because with the budget not approved, the threat of US bonds defaulting surfaced, and this started a little panic.

And this wouldn't be just a local natural disaster like I'd experienced when I'd stood in line outside the Radio Shack door. Within days, the price of silver virtually doubled from around $25 to $50 an ounce. Because this foretold a national, financial, money crisis, and people sensed it. And they started moving towards real money, not government currency backed by debt and promises.
And that real money was silver.

But the crisis continued, and in August, with no satisfactory resolution to the problem, Standard & Poor's actually downgraded the federal government credit rating. The stock market fell 635 points in one day, finally bringing it down 2000 points from just a month before.

Eventually the U.S. Secretary of the Treasury used extraordinary measures to delay the crisis. And the price of silver started dropping back to a new normal of $30 an ounce as many investors unloaded their silver and moved back into stocks.

But it was a real lesson for all of us. And that is that a national financial crisis is possible. And when people panic, they go to real money like silver for security.

So what if there's a real default someday, or a disastrous hacking of the financial system, that spreads around the globe. What if all of the ATM's go dark? What if people lose confidence in US dollars and even cash?

It's something to think about and prepare for. Because what's left? What's one real form of money that people can use and will trust - money that's not dependent on the financial system or the government? And the answer is silver.

Now I'm no conspiracy theorist or extremist. In fact, I lead a pretty normal life, and am somewhat optimistic about the future. But I also believe in planning for disasters. In fact, among other things, I'm a former computer consultant who wrote disaster recovery plans for hospitals.

So that experience, along with the warnings we've gotten from the financial system, and surviving 11 hurricanes in Florida, and has lead me to this point. And that is that we all need to make reasonable preparations to protect ourselves and our loved ones in case a disaster hits.

Which is why I had gotten plenty of cash the day before Hurricane Wilma had hit. And why I buy silver today, in case a financial storm hits. Because silver is part of that preparation, and gives you financial security. And this is one of the greatest reasons to own it.

So with all of that said, maybe we should learn more about this valuable metal. Let's look into some basic information about silver right now.

WHAT ABOUT GOLD?   Note that gold is an important precious metal also. But it's too valuable to be useful for smaller transactions and purchases.

For example, in a financial crisis, at $1200+ per ounce, you couldn't just walk into a grocery store or gas station and use a one ounce gold coin to make a purchase. Even the smallest denomination of gold coin, which is a 1/10 ounce coin, is problematic. Because at $1200+ per ounce, that would still be worth $120 dollars. That's like trying to use $100 bills for small purchases. And worse yet, in a crisis, it might be $10,000 an ounce, which would be like buying groceries with a $10,000 dollar bill.

But silver, which is far lower in price, is readily tradeable. You can think of a one ounce silver coin as a twenty dollar bill (at writing silver is about $17 per ounce). And junk silver dimes, which we'll get into later, are like the proverbial three dollar bill :-). So even if the price explodes, you still have useable denominations of currency.

Now you can't walk into a local Walmart today and buy goods with silver. But in a financial crisis, retailers would be only too anxious to accept an alternative currency like silver coins.

And people would accept them in private transactions too. No doubt millions of people would acquire silver, because they would quickly pick up on its value. After all, silver has been used as money for thousands of years in human history.

So gold will be useful for larger purchases. But silver will be used for everyday transactions to survive. Or put another way, silver can represent money in your pocket. Which is why smart investors should have at least a small portion of their money in silver.

There's a fascinating book on this subject entitled **When the ATMs Go Dark** by Jaclyn Frakes (Author), Bonner & Partners (Author). You can buy it on Amazon at https://www.amazon.com/When-ATMs-Dark-Jaclyn-Frakes/dp/B074Z21BSD/ref=sr_1_1?crid=B2FDL91YSGEL&keywords=when+the+atms+go+dark&qid=1570891482&sprefix=when+the+atms+go+dark%2Caps%2C1503&sr=8-1. Or just go to Amazon.com and search for it by the title.

3

BASIC INFORMATION ABOUT SILVER

Of course we all know what silver is in a general sense. It's a shiny, soft, white, lustrous metal. Indeed, the Latin word for silver is argentum, which means shiny or white. And in fact, the country Argentina, which produces silver, is named after that very Latin word.

But there are many unique things about silver that are not generally known. So we'll look into these because they'll give us insights into why silver is so uniquely useful. And they'll help us with our investments too.

So let's start with the basics. And that is, how is silver measured?

How Silver Is Measured - Weight and Purity

As you deal with silver, you'll focus on two specific measures. And they are its weight, and it's purity (or fineness). So let's start with the weight first.

Silver weight is measured in ounces. But these are not the normal ounces you're used to, like if you're buying a 12 ounce steak at the grocery store. Silver ounces are actually a little bit bigger. And these bigger ounces are known as Troy ounces.

Grams

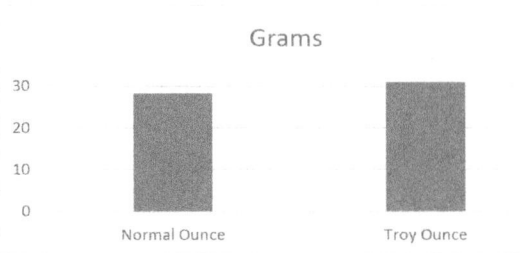

Figure 3-1. Difference between Normal (Avoirdupois) Ounces vs. Troy Ounces

That said, these two different ounce measures are about the same. Just look at the chart comparison above and you'll see what I mean. See, not much difference, is there?

And pardon my bias, but to keep it simple, what I call a normal ounce is actually called an avoirdupois ounce. These normal, avoirdupois ounces are used in many English speaking countries. And a normal ounce is 28.35 grams, but a troy ounce is 31.10 grams.

Okay, great, but what's a gram? Well, a paper clip weighs about a gram. So about 31 paperclips would weigh a troy ounce, and about 28 paperclips would weigh a normal ounce. Or for the food minded, you can use a raisin (about one gram) or a stick of gum (also about one gram).

And then there's an even smaller unit called grains. This is an ancient unit based on a single grain of barley or wheat. And there are 437.5 grains in a normal ounce and 480 grains in a Troy ounce.

And to further confuse the situation, there are 16 ounces in a normal pound, but 12 ounces in a troy pound.

All that said, most of the time you will be dealing with troy ounces. And sometimes troy grams, if you invest in older US coins. For example, the pre-1965 U.S. dime, contains 2.5 grams of silver. So about 14 of these dimes make a Troy ounce of silver (31.10 grams in troy ounce / 2.25 silver grams in dime = 13.82 dimes per troy ounce).

So to summarize…
- There are 12 troy ounces in a troy pound
- There are 31.1 grams in a troy ounce
- And there are 480 grains in a troy ounce

So that's it for weighing silver - mostly in troy ounces and sometimes in grams. This tells you the weight of the silver coins, bars, ingots, etc. that you are buying.

Which leads us to the other important measure of silver, and that is its purity. That is to say, how much of the weight is actually silver, versus other cheaper metals. And unlike other precious investments, this is pretty straightforward (as opposed to karats of gold or carats of diamonds).

Silver purity, also called fineness, is simply measured as a percent of the total weight that is silver. The rest of the weight contains other metals like copper, often added to increase strength and durability. So in our example of a dime above, it is 90% pure silver. So, since the coin weighs 2.5 grams, then the silver content is 2.25 grams (2.5 X .90 = 2.25).

Here's another example of silver fineness. I'm sitting here holding a 1 ounce US Silver Eagle coin. And it says on the coin that it is 1 oz. Fine Silver - which is 99.9% silver. This can also be stated as .999 fine, or "three nines fine." But it all means the same - that it is 99.9% pure silver. That's basically pure silver.

And now, holding a 1 ounce Canadian Silver Maple Leaf coin, it also says Fine Silver. But it also shows a 9999 on the coin. So that is 99.99% silver, or "four nines fine." That's actually "ultra-fine" and about as pure as you can get.

So you really have to hand it to the Canadians on this one, as they clearly take their silver seriously. I love these coins for that reason, and because I can often buy them for a dollar less than the US Silver Eagles (there's less commission on them).

The other silver fineness measure is sterling silver, which is 92.5% silver, or written as 925 or .925. But you won't run into that too often in coins and bars.

So that's it for silver fineness. It's pretty straightforward really. Silver fineness is simply measured as a percent of silver contained in the coin or bar in question.

So with those two key measures established, let's look into the silver prices used in this book and then move on to some other key basics about silver.

My Working Numbers - Gold and Silver Prices

Silver prices change constantly, like any other commodity prices. So when you are reading this book, the silver price is going to be different than when I wrote it.

But no worries, because we're looking at the overall concept of silver investing here. Its just useful to illustrate certain concepts with prices, but we won't get hung up on the exact silver price at the moment.

So here's how I use prices. When I'm referring to a specific time period in **the past**, I will typically use the silver price of that time period.

If I'm talking about more current prices, i.e. **the present**, I often use the following working prices throughout most of the book. For the current gold price I often use $1200 an ounce. For the current silver price, I often use $20 an ounce. And I use $3 as the price of a silver dime (1964 and earlier).

I also discuss possible future prices. Now note that no one knows the future. And there's no guarantee if or when these prices might happen. But history indicates silver could go up pretty dramatically from here, as high as 500% or more over time.

So **the future** prices I use are $100 per ounce for silver and $6000 per ounce for gold. So that gives us a silver / gold ratio, which we discuss later, of 60 to 1. I also use $15 for the future price of a silver dime.

So those are the working numbers in this book. You can always check the exact, at the moment price if you want to. This price is known as the spot price, and it can be found on any number of web sites.

Here's a handy one at www.silver.com. And here's an interesting site that gives the value of silver in grams at http://www.silvergrambars.com/. You can also see the spot prices of gold and silver on the morning CNBC TV show Squawk Box and any number of other financial TV shows.

And finally, to give you a gauge on these working numbers, at writing, on 7/15/18, the prices were as follows. Spot silver was at $15.88, spot gold at

$1243.02, and one gram of silver was $.50 - so a silver dime with 2.25 grams of silver was worth about $1.25. And the silver to gold ratio, which we will get into later, was 78.28 - which made silver a screaming buy.

Okay, so with those guidelines behind us, let's move on to the many important uses of silver. And one of the most important uses, until modern times, has been as money. In fact, silver was "official" money in the US throughout most of its history. And believe it or not, the use of silver was written right into the US Constitution.

Silver As Money In The US

Silver has been "official" money in the US throughout much of its history. That's because the founding fathers were quite serious about having a sound currency for their young nation.

So serious, in fact, that they wrote it into the US Constitution back in 1787. And then they went even further, by passing the Coinage Act of 1792, where they said that a dollar was to be 371.25 grains of fine silver (about 3/4 ounce, worth about $15 today).

Silver (and gold) as Money in the US Constitution:
Article 1 - Section 8 (excerpt): The Congress shall have Power To… coin Money, regulate the Value thereof, and of foreign Coin, and fix the Standard of Weights and Measures;
Article 1 - Section 10 (excerpt) No State shall… make any Thing but gold and silver Coin a Tender in Payment of Debts;
The Coinage Act of 1792: Defined the "dollar" as a weight of silver (371.25 grains (troy) of fine silver) and then *regulated* the value of gold coins to it in a 15 to1 ratio, that is, as 15 grains of silver to every grain of gold.

And for much of US history, the silver (and gold) money was good, honest money that held its value. And the paper currency was good as well.

For example, consider the silver dollar coins, which were 90% silver. Now, that was good, honest money. Of course, for larger transactions, hauling around a bunch of silver coins was pretty unwieldy.

So to make things easier, the US Treasury also printed paper money called dollars. And these dollars looked similar to the dollars we use today, with images of past Presidents on them to make them look official.

But these paper dollars were actually quite different than today's dollars, because they were silver certificates. They actually said "silver certificate" right on the paper dollars. And that meant you could take that paper dollar to a bank, and they would give you a real silver dollar coin for it.

Figure 3-2. Dollars Used To Be Silver Certificates

In other words, that paper dollar was a "claim check" on a real silver coin. So the paper dollars and silver coins were both real money. And the number of dollars the government could print was somewhat limited by the amount of silver (and gold) that it had. So this was a perfectly good, honest system.

Then in the 1930's, during the great economic depression, the government started moving away from the silver and gold standard, and they even made it illegal for citizens to own gold and silver (except for jewelry).

Then after 1964, the government quit making silver coins altogether. They started minting coins out of cheap, base metals. So as the old silver coins disappeared from circulation, there were no silver coins available to exchange the silver certificates for anyway.

And eventually, in August of 1971, they gave up all pretense of backing the US dollar with silver or gold. The dollar bills quit saying "Silver Certificate," and started saying "Federal Reserve Note" instead. And so you couldn't go to the bank and exchange them for silver dollars any more. Instead, the dollar was now just a paper note, not a claim check on real silver.

Do you know what a "note" is? Here's one financial definition of a note. A note is "a legal document that serves as an IOU from a borrower to a creditor." It's an IOU. It's a loan, a debt, backed only by a promise that the government will force other people to use that Federal Reserve Note as money. In other words, we went from a precious metals based currency to a debt based currency.

So now the government didn't have to limit the number of paper dollars they printed to the amount of silver they had. And having dispensed with that pesky silver exchange promise, there was really no limit to how many paper dollars the government could print. Which meant, there was also no limit to how much they could spend, either.

They could just print dollars out of thin air to cover their increased spending.

Which made the value of the dollars go down in value, as we saw in earlier chapters. And the spending increases continue to this day, until we now have a national debt over 20 trillion dollars and counting.

Speaking of counting, here's that US debt clock again - http:// www.usdebtclock.org/. The numbers just fly by as you watch it. It's truly alarming. For example, in the minute I took to write this small factoid, the national debt went up $2,300,000 dollars. Seriously - that happened in one

That's some big IOU. And it's pretty obvious at this point that the dollar is going broke. It's no longer a good store of value. And in fact, this has not just happened to the US dollar. This is going on in most of the world's currencies today as well.

So one of the big uses of silver, as money, has disappeared. But silver's use as a store of value has not. It's stayed the same. But why is that? Why has silver stood the test of time?

Well, it comes down to two things, really. And that is effort and scarcity.

You Can't Just Print More Silver

Unlike paper currencies, the government can't just print more silver. Which is why silver holds its value - because its scarce and hard to come by.

It takes a lot of hard work to find silver ore in the ground, and to mine it. And that silver ore doesn't contain very much silver, either. For example, one of the best silver mines in the world is the Uchucchacua operation in Peru. But their ore only has 445 grams of silver in every ton that they mine.

Think about that. That's just 14 ounces of silver out of 2000 pounds of rock and dirt. That's a lot of rock and dirt to dig up. And then you have to separate the silver out of it with a complicated process, just to get those few, hard won ounces of silver.

And this is at one of the best silver mines in the world.

So that effort and scarcity is why silver has held its value. And even though we don't use it for money anymore, it still continues to be useful as a store of value. And silver has many more uses as well. And they create an increasingly big demand for this precious metal.

Silver Also Has Many Commercial Uses

As I write this chapter, I glance at the silver and gold ring on my finger. And that illustrates an obvious use for silver, which is in jewelry.

But less known is that silver also has many industrial uses, because it has some special properties. And one of these is reflectivity.

Silver has the highest reflectivity of all the metals. So glass mirrors are most often coated with silver (or aluminum). And aside from vanity, there are other mirror applications as well. Like in big solar energy farms, where the silver mirrors reflect the sun's rays into collectors that heat salts used to generate electricity.

And since silver is also the best conductor of electricity, it is often used in modern electronics, in the components such as capacitors, transistors, old and new integrated circuits and chips. For example, one kilogram of certain old transistors used in electronic circuits has up to 20 grams of silver.

And few people know there is silver in computer keyboards as well. As you can imagine, phones and other telecommunication devices also have silver.

Silver is also used in solar panels, and there are about 20 grams of silver used in each panel. So for those interested in green, renewable energy, you simply don't have that type of solar energy without silver. And the use of this application is rapidly growing.

Surprisingly, silver is also used in nuclear energy as well. It's often used in the control rods of nuclear reactors. This is critical, since inserting these silver rods into the nuclear core of a reactor slows down the reaction, while removing them speeds it up. In other words, silver is used to keep control of the reaction - which is a good thing when it comes to nuclear, wouldn't you say.

Silver is also used in the medical industry and has antibacterial properties. It is effective as an antiseptic. It does this by irreversibly damaging key enzyme systems in the pathogen cell membranes. In other words, it kills the bad guy cells.

So now there are silver based bandages. And you can also buy silver-laced toothbrushes, and hairbrushes, combs, make-up applicators, and even silver-based soap.

And the list goes on and on, including water treatment, paper, food processing, photography, x-rays, building materials, wood preservation, textiles, and many other consumer products too numerous to mention. And the number of uses is growing.

So the demand keeps growing too. Which is not surprising when you realize that silver sits in a unique position among the metals. Because it is a precious metal AND an industrial metal. Just look at this simple comparison.

- Gold - Precious metal
- Silver - Precious metal and industrial metal
- Copper - Industrial metal

So silver gets demand from both major uses. But there's another reason for silver demand and scarcity that can drive the price up. And you may have trouble believing this one, because it has to do with the trash.

Silver Gets Used Up - Gold Not

Okay, so silver has many industrial uses and there's an increasing demand for it. But here's something else that sets it apart. And that is that many of these silver products ultimately wind up in the trash and the silver is typically not recovered.

In other words, silver gets used up.

Just think about that. What did you do with your last laptop when you bought a new one? Or your last used Band-Aid - ug. Or your last iPhone?

Contrast this to gold, where almost all of the gold ever mined in human history still exists. That's because gold gets recycled, not used up.

But silver gets thrown away. So there's always a certain replacement demand for it, whether the economy is going up or down. Which means it will continue to be scarce and have value.

And the supply situation has challenges too. Because there are very few primary silver mines in the world. So let's look into that supply side and silver mining.

How Much Gold Is There? By the way, estimates are that all of the gold in the world weighs about 171,000 tons. If that sounds like a lot, it's really not. Because that would be a cube that is only 68 feet tall. Or for you tennis aficionados, it would be a block of gold about the size of the Wimbledon center court and just 32 feet tall (9.8 meters).

Silver Found With Other Metals

As valuable and useful as silver is, companies rarely just mine for silver. This is because silver is usually found with ore containing other metals such as copper, tin, zinc or lead. And silver is also found with gold.

Worldwide, only 6 of the top 20 silver producers are primary silver miners. So only 30% of the annual silver supply comes from primary silver mines. Most of the remainder comes from lead / zinc mines (33%) and copper mines (20%).

This situation is even worse in the United States, where only three mines are primary silver mines, and 39 mines produce silver as a byproduct of gold and base metals.

So here's the key takeaway. Silver is very important to the world economy, with a demand of 1,017,000,000 ounces in 2017. And yet, the majority of it is mined as a secondary byproduct of other mining activities.

Worse yet, the silver ore being mined is getting less dense, and harder to mine.

And they aren't mining enough to keep up. According to the Silver Institute's World Silver Survey 2018, they are coming up short by 26,000,000 ounces per year. That's a pretty big deficit. And where there's a deficit, price increases will eventually follow.

So who's producing the most silver today? Well, it turns out it's our neighbor down south, so let's look into that.

Here's a great resource for you. You can find all kinds of statistics on supply and demand at the Silver Institute Site. http://www.silverinstitute.org

Who's Producing The Most Silver

Rank ♦	Country/Region ♦	Silver production ♦ (tonnes)
—	*World*	38,223
1	Mexico	5,600
2	Peru	4,500
3	China	2,500
4	Russia	1,600
5	Poland	1,400
6	Chile	1,200
7	Bolivia	1,228
8	Australia	1,200
9	United States	1,020

Figure 3-3. List Of Countries By Silver Production (2017)
Courtesy of www.wikipedia.org

So who's producing the most silver today? Well, the largest silver producing country in the world is Mexico, producing 5,600 tonnes per year.

That's over 180,000,000 troy ounces (1 metric tonne x 32150.7466 troy ounces per metric ton = 180,044,181 troy ounces). Also note that metric tonnes are 2204.6 pounds as opposed to US tons of 2000 pounds.

Mexico is followed by Peru (4500 tonnes), China (2500) and Russia (1600).

And the US is 9th on the list at 1020 tonnes. And within the US, the biggest silver producing states, in order, are Alaska, Nevada and Idaho.

Why Silver Instead Of Gold?

You may be wondering why I focus on silver over gold as the precious metal of choice. And the truth is that most investors should have both silver and gold. But I favor silver because it offers the most value for many investors, especially beginning investors.

And it's a good place to start since many beginning investors don't have $1200 to plunk down for an ounce of gold. But they do have $20 to invest in an ounce of silver, or $3 for a silver dime.

And this affordability means they'll be more inclined to invest on a regular basis. Recall our earlier story of teenagers mowing lawns and taking their money to buy silver at the coin dealers. This is why silver is often referred to as the poor man's gold.

But affordability aside, there's another reason to focus on silver over gold. And that's because it seems to be the most undervalued of the two. Which means it has the highest potential for price appreciation. So the chances are better that you can make a lot of money, if and when it's price catches up.

Because in terms of gold, silver is historically very cheap. And we can tell that by simply looking at an important measure called the Gold to Silver ratio.

The Gold to Silver Ratio

A great way to evaluate silver's investment potential is to look at its price in relation to gold's price. This can tell us if silver seems to be undervalued, or overvalued. And we can do this by simply calculating how many ounces of silver it would take to buy an ounce of gold?

So let's do that right now. We'll use our working prices of silver at $20 an ounce, and gold at $1200 an ounce. Then we simply divide the gold price by the silver price. And that shows that it would take 60 ounces of silver to buy just one ounce of gold ($1200 an ounce for gold / $20 an ounce for silver = 60 ounces of silver).

So that gives us a "gold to silver" ratio of 60 to 1.

Silver As Money Is Not Just Theory: By the way, this isn't just some theoretical term and exercise. You really can buy gold with silver in certain circumstances. I recently did just that at my local coin dealer's shop.

I wanted to buy a 1/10th ounce gold Krugerrand coin as a gift. And I gave him 6 one-ounce silver coins as payment for it - plus commission. And that was a 60 to 1 gold to silver ratio (0.10 ounce of gold X 60 = 6 ounces of silver).

Interesting, isn't it. Because I normally pay him dollars, as money, for my precious metal's purchases. But instead, I paid him silver, as money, and he accepted it. And that's because silver is money too, and has been used as such for over 5000 years.

Now let's put that current 60 to 1 gold to silver ratio into perspective. According to the U.S. Geological Survey estimates, there's 17.5 times more silver in the Earth's crust than gold. Let's just make that 17 to keep the numbers simple. So based on the relative scarcity of gold to silver in the earth, the gold to silver ratio should be just 17 to 1.

In other words, I should only have to pay 17 silver coins for an ounce of gold, not 60!
Or when I bought the 1/10th ounce gold Krugerrand above, it should have only cost 2 silver coins (1.7 to be exact) instead of 6 silver coins!

Wow! That's some price difference. The market is treating silver, a precious metal, like it's dirt cheap these days. So it has some real future profit potential.

Here's another fact for you. And that is that historically, prior to 1900, the gold to silver ratio was around 16 to 1. Interesting, isn't it? That's actually pretty close to how scarce gold really is in relation to silver in the earth's crust, at 17 to 1 mentioned above.

However, the more recent average gold to silver ratio over the last century moved it up to 40 to 1. So silver has been trending toward cheaper in relation to gold.

But all that said, what should the gold to silver ratio actually be? Well, the most often quoted number is 16 to 1, because that's what it has averaged for hundreds of years.

So what would that look like if silver went back to that 16 to 1 gold to silver ratio? Let's take an example and see what that means. So let's say you bought 500 ounces of silver for $20 an ounce. That's an investment of $10,000. And that's at our current gold to silver ratio of 60 to 1 (i.e. gold at $1200 an ounce).

And let's say the silver market suddenly became very tight and went to the historical 16 to 1 gold to silver ratio. That would make your $20 silver worth $75 an ounce ($1200 / 16 = $75 an ounce). So then your $10,000 silver investment would suddenly be worth $37,000 (500 x $75 = $37,500).

That's some profit, yes? And even if 40 to 1 became the new normal, your silver would now be worth $30 an ounce instead of $20, for a fifty percent profit.

And here's a final thought for you. And that is that it's pretty easy to make the case for $100 an ounce silver sometime in the future. There are a number of silver experts that predict just that - and even higher. For example, in their seminal book *The Silver Manifesto*, David Morgan and Chris Marchese say, "At some point in the next five years, the price of silver is destined to reach triple-digit prices…".

And in that case, at $100 an ounce, your $10,000 investment would be worth $50,000. And that's a whopping 500% increase and profit.

OK, so that's great in theory, but how is that even possible? And that question leads us to another little known fact about silver. And that is just how small and tight the "available silver" market is.

For The History Buffs: The gold to silver ratio has varied throughout history. Back in Egypt in 3200 BC, silver was highly valued, requiring only 2.5 ounces of silver to buy 1 ounce of gold. But over time, prices gradually approached the 17 to 1 ratio of silver and gold in the earth's crust.

Time Frame / Era	It took This Many Ounces Of Silver	To buy 1 Ounce Of Gold	Gold To Silver Ratio
Egypt, 3200 BC	2.5	1	2.5 to 1
Greece, 445 BC, Plato	12.0	1	12 to 1
Rome, 40 BC, Julius Caesar	7.5	1	7.5 to 1
Medieval England	11.1	1	11.1 to 1
Medieval Italy	12.6	1	12.6 to 1
Germany, 1871 AD	16.7	1	16.7 to 1

Figure 3-4. The Gold To Silver Ratio Through History

Available Silver More Scarce Than Gold

Here's an interesting predicament for you. And that is that the available silver today is more scarce than the available gold. And when something is more scarce, it's price eventually goes up.

You may wonder how silver can be more scarce than gold since geologist tell us there's about 17 times more silver in the earth's crust than gold.

But what we're talking about here is how much silver and gold is actually available to the market. Because it's what's available on the market, not what's in the ground, that influences the price.

And looking at today's silver availability, here's the real situation. The above ground silver reserves are estimated to be only 500 million ounces, compared 2 billion ounces of gold.

Just think about that. Even though gold is much more scarce and expensive, there's four times more of it on the market. So theoretically, gold should be priced at one fourth the price of silver - or silver priced at four times the price of gold.

But instead, gold is priced at 60 times the price of silver. So based on availability on the market, silver prices are way out of line, i.e. way too cheap.

And with demand for silver continuing to rise with more and more industrial uses, that squeeze on available supply could tighten. Remember, there is increased use for solar panels, electric vehicles, larger and more efficient batteries, etc. And we haven't even considered a potential increase in investment silver demand, if inflation begins to rise and investors flee to silver to protect their wealth.

So all things considered, demand should increase over time, while supply is forecast to be at a slight deficit or shortage. And that tight supply and demand could create a precarious unbalance.

And when there's an unbalance, there can be frequent and strong price changes. Which leads to our next topic, that silver prices can be more volatile than gold prices.

Silver Is More Volatile Than Gold - Speculators Dream

Silver investing is not for the faint of heart, because the prices can go up and down dramatically at times. For example, in 2016, gold prices rose 8.1 percent, but silver rose 16 percent according to the London Bullion Market Association.

So silver moved twice as much as gold. In this case, that was a good thing if you owned silver because the price went up. So your silver was worth more. But the reverse can happen too. That is, when the price of gold falls, silver prices tend to fall further.

And not only are the price moves bigger than gold, but they happen much more often. Silver's price movements have been greater than gold's 71.7% of the time. In other words, regardless of the direction on any given day, silver had a greater move percent than gold on roughly three out of four days.

So silver investors need to be tougher than most, so as not to bail out of the market, only to see a big price increase happen right after that.

Which is why it's usually best to buy physical silver first, because you're less likely to sell it during one of these price drops. And this also gets you used to silver's volatility. Then, if and when you buy silver stocks and/or funds, you will be less inclined to panic and bail out at the click of a mouse.

There are times to sell these silver investments of course, but we want to use guidelines instead of emotions when we do that. And we'll get into that later in the book.

But just go into this with your eyes wide open, knowing that silver prices can bounce around. And maybe even use the price drops to add more to your position.

Now, while we're setting expectations, also realize that sometimes the price can just be stable and boring for a while. So if you have silver speculation fever, and expect to buy silver today, and see a big jump in the price tomorrow, you may be disappointed.

So it's best to remind ourselves from time to time that we invest in silver for other reasons besides just price appreciation. We also invest to preserve our purchasing power over time, and we invest as financial insurance too.

And that will keep you in the game, and positioned for any big move that may happen in the future.

4

DIFFERENT TYPES OF SILVER INVESTMENTS

There are many ways to invest in silver. Some are simple and require little time and skill. Others are more complicated, requiring more expertise, time and attention.

Silver coins are the simplest and most popular. These coins are created by official government mints and are highly valued and easy to trade. And that's because the sovereign nations stand behind their content and purity.

Then there are silver rounds (which look like coins), and silver bars. They are created by silver refiners and are also valued for their silver content. They are typically cheaper per ounce, but their content and purity is not backed by a sovereign nation.

These coins, rounds and bars are "physical silver." They are "hold in your hand" silver investments, **and this is where most silver investors should begin.** They are yours, and completely removed from the financial and banking system. So you can view them as financial insurance, as opposed to other financial investments that could be destroyed by a financial system collapse.

There are also silver stocks and stock funds within the financial system. They include silver mining stocks and various funds that hold, or track, the value of silver. These are not physical silver investments, but they tend to go up and down with the price of silver. So they are often referred to as "paper silver" as opposed to "physical silver." And if you have a stock market account, you can buy and sell them with the click of a mouse.

So let's look deeper into these various silver investments. And let's start with my favorite, called silver bullion coins. That's not to be confused with bouillon cubes for soup, although interestingly, the two words are related as you'll see in the next chapter.

Sovereign Silver Bullion Coins

Sovereign silver bullion coins are the most popular and are created by official government mints. These physical, hold in your hand silver coins are also referred to as bullion coins. And with bullion coins, we are strictly interested in their silver content.

This is important to remember when we buy these coins. Because we don't buy them for their scarcity and collectable value. That would just add more cost and complexity to the process.

For example, if a coin that was minted in a certain year is scarce, we don't buy it and pay an extra premium for its scarcity. That scarcity and premium is known as it's numismatic, or collectable value, and that is what coin collectors look for.

But we're not coin collectors. We're buying bullion coins strictly for their silver.

Just think of it like this. If the coins you are buying were melted down, you should have about as much value (strictly the silver content) as if they were not melted down. Indeed, the origin of the Anglo-French term bullion means "boiling," or melted (see, I told you this was related to soup cubes).

There are a number of popular one ounce silver bullion coins that are made by official government mints. So we'll look at seven of the most popular ones.

And of these seven, many experts consider the best, for investment purposes, to be the United States Silver Eagles. So let's start there, with these beautiful coins.

BULLION: Your physical, hold in your hand silver is also called bullion [boo l-yuh n].
1. gold or silver considered in mass rather than in value. 2. gold or silver in the form of coins, bars or ingots.
Origin of bullion: Anglo-Latin, Anglo-French, 1300-1350, 1300-50; Middle English: **melted mass of gold or silver** < Anglo-Latin bulliōn- (stem of bulliō) in same sense (< Anglo-French bullion mint), literally, a boiling, equivalent to bull(īre) to bubble, boil1+ -iōn- -ion, also "place where coins are made.

COIN COLLECTING: Note that there's nothing wrong with coin collecting and buying rare coins for their collectable value. Indeed, for those interested in collecting, this can bring hours of pleasure and pride in their collection.

And coin collecting offers an additional way to make money with the coins as their collectible value can go up in addition to the value of the silver content.

However, writing about the collectable value of the various coins, years, mints, etc. would be an entire book in itself and beyond the scope of this one. But for those interested in coin collecting, you can buy the ***Official Red Book - A Guide Book Of United States Coins*** by R. S. Yeoman. It's available on Amazon and is a fascinating and definitive read.

But we keep it simple here in this beginner's book, and just go for the silver content. And that will serve most readers well. Also, I do not personally buy any coins for their collectable value.

WHAT TO SAY WHEN YOU BUY BULLION COINS: So when you talk to a coin dealer, here is what you say: "I want to buy United States one ounce Silver Eagles (or whatever bullion coin you are buying). *I am buying strictly for the silver bullion content, not the collectable value.*"

United States Silver Eagle

Figure 4-1. United States Silver Eagle

The United States Silver Eagle is the main way I buy silver bullion, and these coins make up about 90% of my physical silver holdings. And at writing you can buy one for about $20 including commission.

These Silver Eagles are the official silver bullion coin of the United States and are produced by the United States mint. The coin was first released on November 24, 1986 and has been produced each year since then.

It's a one ounce silver coin, and this is the only size it's produced in. The coin is guaranteed to contain one troy ounce of 99.9% pure silver by the United States mint. This purity is also often referred to as .999 fine. And the coin is stamped with a one dollar face value (called the nominal value).

The front (obverse) of the coin depicts the Walking Liberty design created by Adolph A. Weinman. It depicts Lady Liberty purposefully striding toward the sun with olive branches in her arm and the American flag draped over her shoulder. And the back (the reverse) features an American eagle, the very symbol of the nation's freedom.

Front or Back; Heads or Tails; Obverse or Reverse: I refer to the two sides of a coin as the front and back just to keep things simple. This is the same as if you were flipping a coin and calling heads (front) or tails (back).

More formal numismatic (coin collecting) terms are the "obverse" (front, heads), because it often depicts the head of a prominent person. And the "reverse" (back, tails).

In fields of scholarship outside of numismatics, the term front is more commonly used than obverse. But the usage of reverse is widespread.

In addition to the bullion version, it's produced in a proof version and an uncirculated version for coin collectors. I don't buy any of these because I'm simply buying the coins for their silver value. I'm also unconcerned with what date they were struck, and don't buy any that are scarce, thereby avoiding paying an additional premium for collector's value.

The Silver Eagle has been produced at three mints, which are the Philadelphia Mint, the San Francisco Mint, and the West Point Mint. Again, I don't care what mint it was produced in - I'm buying strictly for the officially stamped .999 pure silver content.

The main reason I buy American Silver Eagles is that they are one of the most known silver bullion coins in the world. They're trusted by foreign and domestic investors, so there will be no authenticity question if I go to sell or trade them. And the market for them is so strong they are practically a liquid asset.

Also, for US citizens, US minted coins have legal tender status and at law are exempt from confiscation. And they are exempt from the Internal Revenue Service's 1099 reporting. So they are an extremely private investment. Another interesting feature is they can be used to fund an IRA (Individual Retirement Account), although I do not do that.

They are also very affordable. So you can buy them in small or large quantities. At writing, you can buy them for about $20 including commission. So in monetary terms, I view each coin as a twenty dollar bill - which may turn into a $100 bill over time.

Additionally, I think they are beautiful coins. And on a personal note, these make great gifts, which I do from time to time (including great Christmas stocking stuffers).

They're readily available at your local coin dealer or online dealer most of the time, unless people are buying heavily, which happens on occasion. Note that in those cases the premium will be higher.

So after reading through all the different ways to invest in silver, if you just can't decide, you could start with these United States Silver Eagle coins.

Or you can buy my next favorite sovereign silver bullion coin, the Canadian Maple Leaf. Because the Canadians are clearly serious about their silver, and make a wonderful coin as well.

Canadian Silver Maple Leaf

Figure 4-2. Canadian Silver Maple Leaf

Canada issues a beautiful sovereign coin called the Silver Maple Leaf. I love these coins, and often wonder why I don't buy more of them. About 10% of my silver coins are Canadian Maple Leaf's.

The coins come in 1 ounce and half ounce sizes, but I only buy the one-ounce coins. And the Canadians clearly take their silver bullion coins seriously. Because their coins are even more pure than the American Silver Eagles, at .9999 pure silver versus .999 pure.

And that makes them the purest of government-issued silver bullion coins. And better yet, I can usually get them for a dollar less commission than the Silver Eagles, so they are a great value.

The front of the coins show a portrait of Queen Elizabeth II. And there are three versions - a young head version, an old head version, and an older head version. The coin is stamped with a five dollar face value (called the nominal value) and the year of issue is on this side. The back (reverse) of the coin shows the Maple Leaf, from which it gets its name.

I've found the Maple Leafs to be readily available whenever I wanted to buy them, so this is yet another advantage. The coins have been minted since 1988 to present. And they are highly recognizable, like the American Silver Eagles. So they are easy to buy and sell with little authenticity questions to deal with.

And on a personal note, I like the heft of the coins. They are somewhat smaller in diameter, which means they are thicker than the silver eagles. So they have a real solid feel to them.

~~~~~

So the Silver Eagles and Maple Leafs are the two main silver bullion coins I buy.

Of course, the United States and Canada are not the only countries to produce official silver bullion coins. Other countries produce official silver bullion coins as well. And depending on what country you live in, there may be advantages to buying them.

So you may want to look into the official coin of your country. They may be easier to buy and sell locally, or they may offer tax advantages to citizens. And of course, pride in country is a factor too, and there's nothing wrong with that.

Chinese Silver Panda

Figure 4-3. Chinese Silver Panda

China issues a beautiful sovereign silver coin called the Silver Panda. I've never bought one, but have been tempted to quite often. After all, who doesn't love Pandas.

The first Silver Pandas were issued in 1983. And from 1983 to 2015 the coins contained one ounce of silver (31.1 grams). However, in 2016 they switched over to the metric system, and silver Pandas containing 30 grams of .999 pure silver. So they contain just slightly less silver than other troy ounce coins.

The front (obverse) of the coin shows the Chinese Temple of Heaven. And the back displays a panda bear(s) with a different design each year. So the pandas are shown in different poses including sitting, eating and playing.

Their face value is 10 yuan and the coin is highly sought after by investors and collectors. While the market has always been strong, it increased a great deal in 2011 when it became legal for Chinese citizens to own silver coins.

The silver Panda's ever changing and beautiful designs make them popular with collectors. And investors also like them for the higher than expected appreciation this has caused. I have also found them to be readily available, although, as I said, I've not bought one.

Note that the Silver Pandas production, fineness and weight has not always been the same since they were first produced. For example, from 1983 to

1985, they weighed less than an ounce and were only .900 fine silver. Then in 1987 they changed to one troy ounce at .999 fine, more in line with what customers expected. And one other exception to note is that no Pandas were produced in 1986 and 1988.

Austrian Silver Philharmonic

Figure 4-4. Austrian Silver Philharmonic

Austria issues a beautiful sovereign silver coin called the Austrian Silver Philharmonic. It's the most widely distributed silver bullion coin minted within Europe. And it's the only silver coin denominated in euros.

The coins have been minted from 2008 to present. They contain 1 troy ounce of .999 pure silver, and are inscribed with the words "1 Unze Feinsilber," or "1 ounce pure silver." The face value is €1.5 euros.

The front (obverse) of the coin shows the famous pipe organ used by the Vienna Philharmonic Orchestra. And the back displays a group of musical instruments - including four violins and a cello, a harp, a bassoon and a Vienna horn.

The Silver Philharmonic is widely collected in Europe, North America and Japan. And it's produced by the Austrian Mint, the oldest continuously operating mint in the world. Its origins can be traced back to the Crusades in 1194 AD. And the mint's reputation for technical precision gives strong value to the coins they produce.

So finding, buying and selling them is quite easy, although I've never bought them.

United Kingdom Silver Britannia

Figure 4-5. United Kingdom Silver Britannia

The United Kingdom issues a classic sovereign silver coin called the British Silver Britannia. And the Silver Britannia consistently ranks in the top five of preferred sovereign coins, as collectors are attracted to the many different versions of the coin.

The coins have been minted since 1997. However, the 1997 - 2012 coins are only .958 pure silver. But from 2013 going forward, they are .999 pure silver. The Britannia also has a face value of £2 stamped on it.

The front (obverse) shows a portrait of Queen Elizabeth II. And the back (reverse) shows Standing Britannia on all of the Silver Britannia bullion coins of 1998, 2000, 2002, 2004, and 2006. Special designs and variations appear on the 1997, 1999, 2001, 2003, 2005, and 2007 coins. Since then, the Royal Mint seems to have settled on a pattern of alternating the Standing Britannia image and a special design on the back of the coin.

The coin is created by the Royal Mint which has been minting coins for 11 centuries. So the coin is part of a long and remarkable history.

And finally, the .999 pure coins from 2013 on are IRA eligible. And my British friend Gerald, in London, England, tells me if he buys Britannia's that they are exempt from capital gains tax when he sells.

This is because they are legal British tender. So this is a great, in-country advantage, and illustrates why buying the sovereign coin of your nation can make sense.

The British have a long history of silver use in currency. Indeed, their modern currency today is still called the Pound Sterling. The original money was born 1200 years ago around 775 AD. Back then, "sterlings" or silver pennies, were the main currency in Anglo-Saxon kingdoms. 240 of them made one pound in weight and this was a vast fortune in the 8th century.

Mexican Silver Libertad

Figure 4-6. Mexican Silver Libertad

The silver Mexican Libertad coins are considered to be some of the most beautiful silver coins in the world. And they have been minted from 1982 to present.

Unlike most other sovereign silver coins, the Libertad does not show a face value; it shows only a weight. The coins contain .999 pure silver, and they're issued in many sizes, ranging from 1/20 oz, 1/10 oz, 1/4 oz, 1/2 oz, 1 oz, 2 oz, 5 oz, 1 kg.

The front (obverse) of the coin shows the Mexican National Seal with an eagle on top of a cactus, holding a serpent in its beak. The eagle is surrounded by a wreath, which is then surrounded by the official name of Mexico in Spanish, "Estados Unidos Mexicanos."

The back (reverse) of the coin shows important symbols of the Mexican people, which are the Angel of Independence and the Mexican volcanoes Popocatépetl and Iztaccíhuatl.

Mexico has a long history with silver, and the Libertad coin is minted by the Mexico Mint, which was established in 1535 by the Spanish Crown. This created the first mint in the Americas, and it has continued to strike great silver and gold bullion coins ever since.

Australian Silver Kookaburra

Figure 4-7. Australian Silver Kookaburra

Australia issues a beautiful and interesting sovereign silver coin called the Kookaburra (you'll also see other coins like the Kangaroos, Koalas, etc.). The coin is named after a bird native to Australia, and the bird image changes every year. This change, along with limited production of the one ounce coins, gives them a higher collectible value than some other bullion coins.

The coins have been minted since 1990. And they were .999 pure silver until 2018 when they increased the purity to .9999 silver. The face value for the one ounce coin is A$1 (one Australian dollar) backed by the federal government. The coin is also issued in 2 and 10 troy ounce sizes, as well as a large 1 kilogram size (2.5 pounds).

The front (obverse) in the 2013 design shows two juvenile kookaburras sitting on a tree branch amid flowers. The back (reverse) shows a likeness of Her Majesty Queen Elizabeth II.

The coin is created by the Perth Mint and is their longest-running silver coin.

Final Thoughts On Bullion Coins

We just looked at seven different silver sovereign bullion coins that you can buy. And sovereign coins like these are the best place to start for most beginners. Now, if you just can't decide which ones to buy, then go with the US Silver Eagles, or Canadian Maple Leafs. Both coins are popular and widely recognized around the world.

And finally, remember, you're just buying them for their silver content.
- You're not buying them for their collectable value.
- You don't care what year they were minted or how scarce they are.
- You're not buying uncirculated coins.
- You're not buying commemorative coins.
- You're not buying proof coins (using special dies to give sharper designs).
- You avoid all of these factors that add cost or complexity to your purchase.

Instead, you just keep it simple and buy them strictly for their silver content. And for their high quality too, which is backed by their national governments.

That said, there's another type of government issued coins for those who want to diversify their silver coin investment. And these coins are called "junk silver." Now that seems like quite a shift from high quality sovereign coins, doesn't it? But there's value in this junk, as you shall see.

Junk Silver Coins

Junk silver coins are my other favorite way to invest in physical silver. And yes, it sounds a bit odd that I like a "junk" silver. But don't be fooled by the name, because these coins are anything but junk.

Junk silver coins are old US currency coins minted before 1965, when the government issued coins containing silver. Specifically, they are any US dime, quarter, or half dollar showing a date of 1964 or before.

And all of these coins contain 90% silver. Contrast that to today's coins, which are made of cheap base metals, and perhaps we should be calling our current coins junk instead.

OTHER JUNK COINS: Note that Kennedy half dollars from 1965–1970 contained 40-percent silver. And there are other coins minted by the US with precious metals, such as silver dollars. But we'll just stick with the typical US dimes, quarters and half dollars, as they are the most common.

Also note that other countries have junk silver coins as well. Some of these are the United Kingdom, Canada and Australia.

So why are these silver coins called junk? Well, since there are over 13 billion of them throughout the country, most of them are not particularly scarce from a collector's point of view. And since the last ones were minted in 1965, they probably show some wear, so again, nothing collectable here.

So they're called junk from a collectors point of view. But these coins are popular among people seeking to invest in silver. And that's because they offer some unique advantages.

Advantages Of Junk Silver Coins

A big advantage of junk silver coins is that they are **easily recognized** because they are old US currency coins. So it's unlikely anyone is going to question their authenticity, or need to assay them for their silver content. They are a known quantity.

And since the coins are US currency, they also have a **floor value**. For example, a pre-1965 dime is still worth ten cents by law, no matter what the value of its silver content. Of course, ten cents is a lot lower than the value of the silver in that dime ($1.25 at a spot price of $17.00 per ounce). But still, there is a floor value.

And since junk silver is US **legal tender**, it's unlikely that these silver coins will be confiscated by the government, like they did with gold back in Franklin Roosevelt's presidency. Note that I said unlikely, but not impossible, because there's just no telling what the government will do. But still, probably unlikely.

Also, in times of financial crisis, these coins, such as dimes, could serve as **small denominations** to be exchanged for goods you really need to survive. For example, if silver went to $100 an ounce in a crisis situation, a junk dime would be worth $7.34 (.07234 troy oz of silver X $100 per oz = $7.234 per dime).

That's a useful denomination of change, kind of like a five or ten dollar bill today. And any merchant would be able to accept it, sell you goods and make change. By contrast, a one ounce silver coin, like a US Silver Eagle, at $100 an ounce, would be like using a hundred dollar bill. So you would only use those coins for larger purchases.

Another advantage to junk silver is the **cheap price** if you can buy in quantity. You can buy bags of these coins in bulk and they will only cost you a few percentage points over the spot silver value.

And finally, you can buy in **quantities that fit your budget**. You can buy half bags, quarter bags and tenth bags. And if you have a tight budget, some coin dealers will sell the coins individually.

So all that said, let's look into the specific quantities and types of junk silver we can buy.

What Kind Of Junk Silver Coins Can I Buy

Junk silver is sold in bags of dimes, quarters or half dollars, and typically these coin denominations are not mixed. So you are either buying a bag of all dimes, or a bag of all quarters, or a bag of all half dollars.

And you can buy bags of coins in different sizes. The size is stated as a face value, and this tells you the number of coins in the bag.

For example, if you're buying a bag of dimes with a face value of $100, then it contains 1000 dimes (10 dimes per dollar X $100 face value bag = 1000 dimes). And those 1000 dimes contain 71.5 ounces of silver.

Using the face value of a bag is handy because it works just the same with the other coin denominations. For example, if you bought a $100 face value bag of quarters, then it would contain 400 quarters. And those 400 quarters would also contain 71.5 ounces of silver.

Similarly, a $100 bag of half dollars would contain 200 coins, which also contain 71.5 ounces of silver. So using the face value makes the bags interchangeable and the pricing the same.

Of course, you will pay much more than $100 for these bags because the coins are 90% silver. So if silver is at $20 an ounce, that would be $1430 worth of silver ($20 an ounce X 71.5 ounces = $1430).

That $1430 is also known as the melt value, which is the value of the coins based on the metals contained within them. Like if you melted the coins down to get the silver (not recommended).

Typically, these bags have been sold to contain $1000 face value of coins. But as you can see in our example above, some dealers sell smaller bags, like the $100 bags we just described. They may also sell half bags ($500) face value and one fourth bags ($250). But note that the smaller bags have a higher commission.

Note that when these coins were minted, they actually contained 72.34 ounces of silver, instead of 71.5 ounces. But over the years it's been agreed that the coins have lost some of their silver due to normal wear and tear. So to compensate for that loss, the silver markets have set the standard at 0.715 ounces of silver for each face value dollar, or 71.5 ounces for our $100 face value bag of coins.

And some coin dealers will sell individual coins as well. For example, I've been able to buy single dimes (my favorite denomination) for $2.50 to $3.00 each. So this is what I mean when I say anyone can get started for three dollars.

So often when I visit my coin dealer and buy some Silver Eagles for $20 each, I throw in a few single silver dimes too. Now those silver dimes only contain about $1.25 in silver. And I'm paying up to $3.00 for them.

So you may be thinking I'm being pretty inefficient with those purchases, and you would be right. But my thinking here is that I want to own some smaller silver denominations in case there is a financial crisis in the future. And I don't want to spend all of the money for a full or fractional bag. So better to at least accumulate some dimes, even at a high markup, than none at all.

Similarly, buying single coins makes it possible for people on a limited budget to at least get started owning silver. Again, because it's probably better to buy a little at a time, at a high markup, than to never buy any at all. And just about anyone can start their silver investment with $3.00 here and there.

But the quantities you buy are up to you and what fits your budget. And the coins you choose are up to you as well. So let's look at the dimes, quarters and half dollars right now.

Junk Dimes

Figure 4-8. Winged Liberty Head Mercury Dime

I tend to buy the junk silver dimes instead of quarters or half dollars, but the choice is yours. There are three types of junk silver dimes and they all contain 90% silver (except for some Roosevelt dimes). And they are, with their years of issue...

- Liberty Head "Barber" (1892–1916).
- Winged Liberty Head "Mercury" (1916–1945) – shown above.
- Roosevelt (1946–1964) -- Roosevelt dimes after 1964 do not contain 90-percent silver.

I prefer the Mercury Dimes (pictured above) because some of the Franklin dimes contain silver and some don't, depending on the year. But there is no question about the silver content of the Mercury dimes.

Junk Quarters

Figure 4-9. Washington Quarter

There are three types of junk silver quarters. The most common junk quarter is the Washington quarter pictured above. All quarters contain 90% silver - except the Washington quarter. Only those Washington quarters issued through and including 1964 contain 90% silver.

The junk quarters with their years of issue are...

- Liberty Head "Barber" (1892–1916).
- Standing Liberty (1916–1930).
- Washington (1932, 1934–1964) – shown above.

Junk Half Dollars

Figure 4-10. Franklin Half Dollar

There are four types of junk half dollars. Pictured above is the Franklin half dollar. All of these half dollars contain 90% silver - except the Kennedy half dollars minted in 1965 - 1970. They only contain 40% silver.
The junk half dollars with their years of issue are...

- Liberty Head "Barber" (1892–1915).
- Walking Liberty (1916–1947).
- Franklin (1948–1963) – shown above.
- Kennedy (1964).
- Kennedy (1965–1970) -- 40-percent silver.

Final Thoughts On Junk Coins

So to sum it all up, buying junk coins is another way to accumulate physical silver. Not only do the coins contain 90% silver, but they are real US government currency. Also, they're recognized around the world and you can get them in various denominations.

Over time they can preserve you purchasing power, and even make you money should the price of silver jump up. And they just might come in handy to buy necessities for you and your family should a financial crisis ever happen.

Buying them by the bag is the most price efficient. But that can be a pretty heavy cost for those starting out. So you can buy fractional bags for less cost. Or even single coins, like a dime, for under $3, which lets just about anyone get started in silver investing.

But there's another way to buy silver even cheaper if you don't want to pay for the benefits of coins. And that's to buy silver bars.

Silver Bars

Silver is also produced in bars, and these are quite popular. That's because they have lower premiums than government minted coins, so you get more silver for your money.

The bars are produced by the silver refiners, and if you buy them from the major refiners, they are easily tradeable and very liquid.

Some of the major refiners are…
- Royal Canadian Mint
- Johnson Matthey
- Republic Metals Corporation
- Engelhard
- Silvertowne
- Pamp Suisse
- Sunshine
- Asahi

Silver bars come in many sizes. The most common you will see are 1 ounce, 10 ounce and 100 ounce bars. And then there's the 1000 ounce "mother of all silver bars" just to get your attention.

So let's look at these popular sizes. And keep in mind that like most bulk buying situations, the bigger the size, the lower the premium per ounce, and the more silver you get for your money.

1 Ounce Silver Bars

Figure 4-11. One Ounce Silver Bar

These are the most affordable to small and beginning investors and are a convenient way to invest in silver. They stack and store well in compact places because of their shape and size, and they are easily transported.

They are produced by most of the major refiners and mints and are made of at least .999 (or 99.9%) pure silver.

They are also easy to buy and sell.   And they're very price efficient, at about $.50 to $1.00 over the spot price of silver. Compare that to the higher $2 to $4 premium for a US Silver Eagle, which is also one ounce of silver.

So at a silver price of $17 an ounce, one of these bars would cost about $18 with the small commission. So I tend to think of them like a twenty dollar bill, as I do with the Silver Eagles.

New investors will often start their silver investment with these small, affordable bars. I did the same years ago for my first physical silver investment. And while I no longer own any, there are seasoned investors who have an ample supply of them to take advantage of their divisibility and liquidity.

So if you prefer to invest in silver bullion for convenience and affordability, these bars are a good way to do it at a good price.

10 Ounce Silver Bars

Figure 4-12. Ten Ounce Silver Bar

10 ounce bars are also produced by most major refiners and mints and are made of at least .999 fine silver. And they are also a convenient way to invest in silver, store and stack well, and are easily transported.

Weighing in at over half a pound (0.685), they have some heft to them. And this is one of the pleasures of investing in physical silver. Because when you pick up a silver bar like this, you feel like you really have something of solid value in your hands.

They are also very price efficient, at about $.50 to $1.00 over the spot price of silver. So with the spot price of silver at $17 an ounce, one of these including a dollar per ounce commission would cost around $180.

Actually, it could be a bit cheaper per ounce than the one ounce bar. So if the one ounce bars were going for $18 an ounce including commission, the ten ounce bar might go for something like $17.90, so $179 or better for the ten ounce bar. And if you buy in quantities of ten or more, you can get even slightly better prices.

100 Ounce Silver Bars

Figure 4-13. 100 Ounce Silver Bar

I've never bought any of the 100 ounce bars, although I'd like to own some just for fun. I've always visualized having one as a cool doorstop.

They are also made of at least .999 fine silver. And they're also a convenient way to invest in silver, store and stack well, and are easily transported.

The typical 100 oz bar is about 6.5 inches long, 2.5 inches wide, and 1.25 inches deep.
Weighing in at almost seven pounds (6.85 of a pound), they have some serious heft to them. So if you pick one of these up, you will feel like your handling something of serious weight and value.

And with the spot price of silver at $17 an ounce, one of these would cost around $1800. Actually, the reduced commission could make it a little cheaper than that. So if the one ounce bars were going for $17.90 an ounce including commission, the 100 ounce bar might go for something like $17.80, so instead of paying $1800 you might pay only $1780 or better. And if you buy in quantities of ten or more, you get even slightly better prices.

They are also made by most of the major refiners and mints.

But the Canadians really shine in the value department here. 100 ounce bars by the Royal Canadian Mint are .9999 pure, versus most other bars at .999 pure. So they really represent a more cost effective way to invest in silver from a globally recognized refiner.

And even with their extreme purity, they don't seem to cost much more. You'll recall a similar situation we saw with the one ounce silver Canadian Maple Leaf coins. I mentioned they were also .9999 pure and I'm able to buy them for a dollar less than the silver American Eagles at .999 pure.

So to my way of thinking, the Canadians really take their silver seriously. And if I were to buy 100 ounce silver bars, I would definitely look into the Royal Canadian Mint bars.

1000 Ounce Silver Bars

Figure 4-14. 1000 Ounce Silver Bar
Image courtesy of Wikipedia at https://en.wikipedia.org/wiki/Silver

Okay, just for fun, 1000 ounce silver bars are available for purchase too. Weighing in at around 70 pounds, these are the mother of all silver bars. Their physical size is 13" x 4 3/4" x 3 1/2". So to visualize one, just think of a really heavy loaf of bread (or a weird, regular weight Christmas fruitcake - chuckle).

Unlike the other bars, these are cast, so their weight is not an exact 1000 ounces and varies considerably. So each must be individually weighed and stamped.

I've never bought one and don't think they will be commonly bought and sold by readers of this book. They're more of a convenient size for industrial purposes.

And they're also popular with very large silver bullion investors, since they can buy silver this way at very close to the market "spot" price. Like the purchase of 100 million ounces by the Hunt Brothers in early 1980. Or Warren Buffett's 129 million ounce Berkshire Hathaway purchase 17 years later (note that he has since sold that position).

Anyhow, back to their weight, combined with packaging, they may well weigh more than the 70 pound flat rate post office limit. Not to mention that one would cost around $17,000 at a spot rate of $17 an ounce. So for most of us, these bars are probably not so easy to buy and sell.

To sum it up, they are less easy to deliver, inexact weight, bulky and heavy, and cost around $17,000. What's not to like about all of that?

Still, for big buyers of physical silver wanting to buy in bulk at the best rate, this is probably the cheapest per ounce silver you can buy.

And I must say, the 1000 ounce bars are impressive, don't you think?

Silver Rounds

Silver rounds are coins, but they are not official government bullion coins or money or legal tender. They are produced by major refiners just like the silver bars. And aside from the fact that they are round instead of rectangular, I consider them to be about the same thing.

The main reason you buy them is to pay a lower premium, just like you buy silver bars to pay a lower premium. And the prices of both are about the same.

Like silver bars, they are the most affordable to small and beginning investors and are a convenient way to invest in silver. They stack and store in compact places because of their shape and size, and are easily transported.

I bought some of these when I first started silver investing, although I no longer own any of them, and stick to American Eagles and Canadian Maple Leafs. But there's nothing wrong with investing in them if you're going for the most silver for your dollar.

They are produced by most of the major refiners and mints and are made of at least .999 (or 99.9%) pure silver. They are also easy to buy and sell. And like silver bars, they are very price efficient, at about a dollar over the spot price of silver. So with the spot price at $17 an ounce, you could buy one of them for around $18.

Be sure you are buying pure .999 silver rounds, because there are some that are just silver clad. So any rounds you see advertised that are lower than the spot price of silver are either clad or not of .999 purity, so stay away from them.

Also, there are all kinds of specialty, novelty and artsy types of silver rounds. I would stay away from most of them as well because you want to buy something that is recognized by future buyers.

One silver round that stands out is the Sunshine Mint Silver Buffalo round.

Figure 4-15. Silver Buffalo Round

It shows a native American Indian on the front, and an American Bison on the back. And it has a special trademarked security feature on it. This is Sun-

shine's MintMark SI anti-counterfeit technology. It works with a (Decoder Lens, sold separately for under $20.

This decoder lens will validate all Sunshine Mint products that contain the MintMark SI security feature. By holding the lens to the circular MintMark it will reveal a "Valid" marking for authentic coins.

Note that the Sunshine Mint is a private firm based in Idaho that handles the processing of silver, gold, and other precious metals. The mint is famous for its silver blanks that it provides to the United States Mint, and is also a highly regarded manufacturer of private silver and gold bullion.

That said, if you prefer to invest in silver bullion in the form of rounds instead of bars, these are a good way to do it. Because to me, bars and rounds are pretty much the same thing.

Just For Fun - Silver Bullet

Figure 4-16. Silver Bullet

Okay, so I cautioned against buying specialty, novelty and artsy types of silver in the last chapter. And that's because you want to buy silver that's recognized by buyers, in case you sell in the future.

But when I saw a silver bullet at my local coin dealers some years ago, I couldn't resist.

You're probably familiar with the term silver bullet, which has become a metaphor for a simple, seemingly magical solution to a difficult problem.

And you'll recall the Lone Ranger western TV series, and how he used a silver bullet as a calling card. The bullets were his symbol for justice, law and order. And also to remind himself that life, like silver, was precious and not to be wasted.

So in deference to the Lone Ranger, and because I could use a magical solution from time to time, of course I bought one.

What the heck, nothing says we can't have a little fun along our investing journey. And aren't we all looking for a magical solution to difficult problems, a silver bullet, in one form or another.

That said, just don't get carried away with these novelties. And aside from this one small transgression, all of my other silver is in official, recognizable form. Also please note that this is just an inert, bullet shaped piece of silver. It is not something that would actually work in a firearm.

Final Thoughts On Silver Bullion

So those are the main ways to invest in physical silver bullion. To summarize, most people will do well to buy their bullion in US Silver Eagles or Canadian Silver Maple Leafs. I buy both, although mainly Silver Eagles.

Or you may want to buy the sovereign coin of your country, if they have one. And if there are special tax advantages to doing so.

It's also good to buy junk silver coins if you like. I buy a few loose junk silver US dimes from time to time. Like I said, I'm very price inefficient by doing this. But I just don't feel like springing for the cost of a full bag. And loose dimes are under $3 each, so this is a way that just about any beginning investor can get started.

Both of these investment types have their authenticity guaranteed by the government, so they are easily tradeable. But the disadvantage is the commissions are typically higher.

For those wanting to be the most price efficient, silver bars and rounds are the way to go. The commission is less, but the tradeoff is they have less of an authenticity guarantee. So they may be a little less tradeable. But many of the major refiners are well recognized, so this is not a major drawback.

All that said, most investors will be well served to have some physical silver as part of their investment portfolio. So physical silver is the place to start.

Then once you've done that, there's another way to invest in silver if you want to go further. Because the value of these silver investments can move even more, and faster, than the price of the silver itself.

And these investments are just a mouse click away. Because we're talking about investing in silver online through the stock market.

Silver Mining Stocks

So let's say you've bought and accumulated some physical silver at this point. If you hold tight right there, you're ahead of most investors. But if you want to go beyond that, you can also invest in silver related stocks and funds. The advantage to this type of silver investing is that you can buy and sell instantly, online, at the click of a mouse. And when the silver price is rising, some of these investments can go up even faster than physical silver.

Of course, when the price of silver is going down, they can go down even faster and lower too. Also they are subject to risks like any other stocks and funds. And you will need a stock investing account to invest in them.

But all that said, I think many will find silver stock and fund investing worth doing because the profit potential can be good over time. So for that reason, I do stock and fund investing along with physical silver investing.

The most obvious way to invest in silver stocks is to invest in silver mining companies. So we'll start off looking at silver mining stocks. Which means you could be owning part of a silver mine. So get your picks and shovels ready, because that sounds pretty exciting, right?

Well, maybe not so much. Because there's quite a bit to consider.

In theory, silver mining is pretty simple. You just go get some land you think has silver in it, dig a hole and take the silver out.

Of course, silver mining is a lot more complicated than that. Because after you start digging, you may find out that your mine has no silver at all. Or maybe very little silver.

And even good silver mines are hard work, because many of them only get around 10 ounces of silver from a ton (2000 pounds) of ore. So they have to move tons of rock to get any worthwhile amount of silver.

And speaking of rock, since silver is typically embedded in it, you have to use explosives to break it up. So that's kind of dangerous. And then there can be some pretty nasty substances like cyanide and mercury involved to separate the silver from the broken rock.

It's estimated that between 1860 and 1889, more than 20.5 million pounds of mercury was used just in the huge silver strikes in the Comstock Lode in western Nevada. Also, speaking of mercury, it's often called "quicksilver," because of its color and liquid mobility.

And some silver mines can be pretty dodgy, too. Particularly the smaller, junior miners. Because many such mines always seem to be short of cash. So to keep operating, they make exaggerated claims of how much silver they have in the ground to get people to invest in them.

Which reminds me of what Mark Twain said, that "a mine is a hole in the ground with a liar standing next to it." So beware, because unless you've really done some serious research, you could invest in a fraudulent mine.

And even if you're investing in a legitimate mine, most of them don't pay a dividend. So you're speculating and your money is just sitting there as you hope they strike big. And the odds of you hitting big are low, although when you do, it can be pretty dramatic and profitable.

I've never hit big in silver mining stocks, but I did once in a junior gold mining stock in the past, called ATAC Resources Limited (ATADF). They hit a rich gold deposit, and the stock went from $.25 to $8.00 in 19 weeks. And most of that price jump happened in just one week. So I made a whopping 1400% on that stock trade.

So you really can go boom or bust in the junior miners. In this case it was boom — as in sonic boom! Here's a chart of what that rocket ride looked like back in 2010…

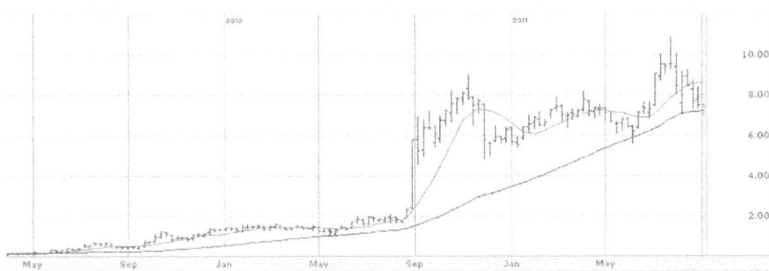

Figure 4-17. A Junior Mining Stock Rocket Ride - ATAC Resources

However, that is the ONLY mining stock I've ever made money that quickly on. And as a cautionary tale, the stock eventually dropped to virtually nothing (16 cents per share at writing). Here's what it looks like today.

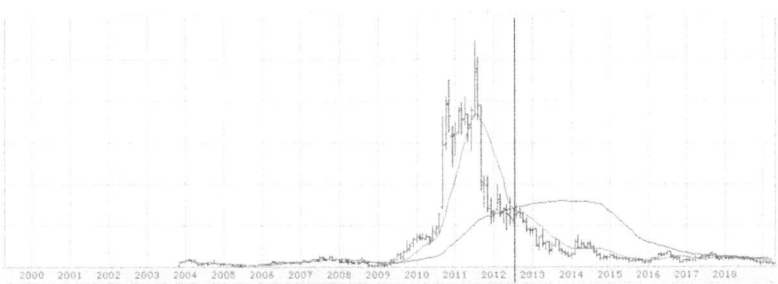

Figure 4-18. ATAC Resources Some Years Later

So if you invest in silver mining stocks, you might consider going with the major miners that have been around for a while. Let's look at three of them, which are Pan American Silver (PAAS), First Majestic Silver (AG) and Endeavor Silver (EXK).

PAAS - Pan American Silver

Pan American Silver (PAAS) is one of the largest silver producers worldwide. The mining company is headquartered in Vancouver, Canada, and they were founded in 1994.

They have mines and other projects in Mexico, Peru, Bolivia and Argentina. And while their primary focus is on silver, they also sell the gold, copper, lead and zinc they discover along with the silver they find. So overall, silver makes up 45% of their revenues, gold 26%, with copper, lead and zinc rounding out the balance.

They have an affordable share price, which has ranged from $13 to $19 per share over the past three years. And 46% of their stock is held by institutions. When a stock has high institutional ownership, that is often a good sign. It can indicate that the smart money, like large investment banks, mutual funds and pension funds, feel the company is doing well.

As mentioned earlier, silver investments typically do not pay a dividend and are speculative investments. What sets PAAS apart from the crowd is they pay a 1.11% dividend. That's pretty rich, when you consider the average dividend paid by US corporations is 1.8%, and most silver miners pay no dividend at all.

Their cost to produce silver is around $10 per ounce. So with silver around $17 per ounce, the company is profitable. The company also has development mines that it expects will increase its production. And it has low debt. You can find their website at https://www.panamericansilver.com/.

So PAAS is one of the best of breed silver stocks out there. They seem well established, produce at a profit, and pay you to invest with their dividend. So your investment is not just dead money waiting for a big jump in the price of silver. Also, I have owned PAAS in the past, but don't own it at writing.

AG First Majestic Silver

First Majestic is a relatively small mining company headquartered in Vancouver, Canada and founded in 2002. The company has six mines all located in Mexico. They are very focused on silver, with over 60% of their revenues coming from silver. Another 24% comes from gold, with lead and zinc making up the rest.

They have an affordable share price of $6.14 per share. The price has been quite volatile since making a 2011 high near $25 per share, and tumbling as far down as $2.66 per share before moving back up to $6.14. 22% of their shares are held by institutions, so someone has faith in their future. They pay no dividends and have fairly low debt (15%). Their company website is at - first-majestic.com

Their cost to produce silver in 2018 was as high as 15.83 per ounce so the company was not profitable. So this is a highly speculative investment, betting on things improving.

How so? They have a number of expansion programs that could nearly double future production. And they have fairly low debt (15%). So that coupled with costs coming down as their scale increases could cause the price to explode in the future as investors catch on. A rise in the price of silver could increase that as well.

So they have potential as a speculative growth stock. What I like about them is that at writing, Wheaton Precious Metals Corp (WPM), a world class royalty company, was involved in a deal with them. So that gives some credence to their future profitability.

I have never owned the stock, but recently took a small position buying 2 year stock options. By the way, this is a highly speculative trade. By that I mean "probably kiss your money goodbye," kind of trade, so I don't recommend it for beginners.

But I have included First Majestic Silver here to show the range of investment and risk out there in the silver mining companies.

EXK - Endeavour Silver Corp

Endeavor Silver Corp is a small, $282 million mining company also headquartered in Vancouver, Canada. It owns four high-grade, underground, silver-gold mines in Mexico, and it also has a good pipeline of exploration and development projects.

About 60% of Endeavor's revenues come from silver and the rest from gold.

The company was founded in 1981, and its share price is an affordable $2.17 a share at writing. Like most mining operations, the company does not pay dividends to its shareholders. Institutions hold 26% of its shares. And the company website can be found at - https://www.edrsilver.com

Endeavor's cost to produce silver was $15.87 in the third quarter of 2018, so with the silver price not much higher, the company wasn't making money. The company has continued to optimize mining methods, and some of their cost is due to development, but Endeavor will need a higher silver price to start turning a profit.

Given that silver is at an extreme low today, the odds are that the price will eventually go up. And Endeavor can probably sustain itself until then because it has zero long-term debt.

I have never owned the stock, and it is higher risk than the other two. However, along with its four operating mines, one development project, and four additional exploration efforts underway and higher price of silver, investors may be rewarded with higher share prices if it moves into profitability.

But all that said, I seldom invest in individual silver mining companies, and don't think they are particularly great for beginning investors. I've included them here just to show you the full spectrum of silver investing.

But silver mining is risky. And investing in a single mining company carries that risk.
Fortunately, there's a better way to invest in mining companies. And that's to invest in silver streamer and royalty companies.

Get Paid With Silver Streamers And Royalty Stocks

One of my favorite ways to invest in silver mining is to invest in silver streamer and royalty companies. I think you'll appreciate their unique way of doing business.

Because these guys **make financial arrangements with the mining companies to get a piece of the action, and then let them do all of the hard work.** So if they are a royalty company, they just take a percent of the mine's revenue as a royalty payment. Or if they are a streamer, they take a portion of their mined silver at a very low price.

Better yet, some of them pay you a dividend too, and what's not to like about that?

So let's take a look at one of my favorite silver streamer, which is Wheaton Precious Metals.

WPM - Wheaton Precious Metals

Wheaton Precious Metals (WPM) is the world's largest silver streaming company, formerly known as Silver Wheaton (SLW). And if you have a stock investing account, you can invest in them with the click of a mouse.

And here's what they do for you as an investor. Wheaton does the serious research to find the best mines out there. So while you and I are going along, living our daily lives, Wheaton is doing that complicated research for us. It's what they do.

Then they make good deals with these mining companies to buy part of their silver for a ridiculously low price. For example, with the price of silver today at around $17 an ounce, they may contract with a mining company to buy 20% of all the silver they mine for $4 an ounce. For the life of the mine! And that may include any new discoveries in the mine too.

That's kind of like someone telling you, "Hey, if you give me four dollars, I'll give you seventeen." It's a good deal if you can get it.

So then Wheaton just takes delivery of the silver every month, at $4 an ounce. And they sell it on the market for $17, and pocket the $13 profit. They're letting someone else do all that hard work, and getting their silver for a song. Like I said, it's good work if you can get it.

There are all kinds of technical variations on how these streamer deals are made. For example, agreements may be based on Net Smelter Return, or Net Royalty Interest, or Net Profit Interests. And rights to purchase in future mines, at varying per cents and prices. The list goes on and on.

But we won't get all hung up on that, and instead just focus on the big concept. Which is that they make up-front deals with miners to get silver (and other precious metals) on the cheap.

About now, you're probably wondering why a mine operator would agree to giving up some of their hard-earned silver, or revenue, to a company like Wheaton?

And that's because Wheaton gives them money up front to help finance their operations. And since silver mining is expensive, and many mining companies are strapped for cash, they find it beneficial to sell some of their future silver or revenue to get that financing.

So, having gotten the financing and cash they need, the mining companies promise some of their future stream of silver to companies like Wheaton in exchange. By the way, you notice that I just used the phrase "future stream of silver." So that's why companies like Wheaton are called silver streaming companies, or streamers.

For fun, go ahead and Google "silver streaming companies." You'll see many entries come back, and some of them will refer to Wheaton Precious Metals, or their older name Silver Wheaton. And you'll see this concise definition at Wikipedia too…

"Silver streaming is the term often used when a company makes an agreement with a mining company to purchase all or part of their silver production at a low, fixed, predetermined price to which both parties agree."

There's another reason why some mining companies will part with some of their hard-earned silver as well. And that's because silver is often a by-product of mining for other metals, such as gold, copper, lead and zinc. For example, about 35% of silver comes from lead and zinc mines. And approximately 10% comes from gold mines. And another 20% from copper mines. The rest comes from primary silver mines.

By the way, as mentioned earlier, there's another, similar type of company called a royalty company. Roughly speaking, the royalty company gets the mining company to agree to pay them part of their revenue (i.e. money). A streaming company gets the mine to pay them in the physical metal (i.e. silver) at a low price.

And some companies do both. So I tend to just treat these as the same type of investments, although there are subtle differences. But we'll just keep using the term streamers to keep it simple.

So it's often the case that these miners just don't want to deal with the silver, because it's not their core business. It's not what they are mining for, or set up to deal with. So they're happy to cheaply sell off their silver to streaming companies to be done with it and get the extra income. And of course, the silver streamers, and us, the investors, are happy to take all of that pesky, bothersome silver off of their hands (big grin).

So silver streaming companies seem to be a great way to go when investing in silver. Because they do all of the research to find the good mines for us. And that lowers our risk.

And they make agreements with a number of different mines. So we don't have all of our eggs in one basket. And they make profitable deals.

And here's another advantage. A common complaint about investing in silver (and other precious metals) is that it's just speculation and dead money - there's no return on it.

But some streamer and royalty companies pay dividends. So we're paid to invest in them while we wait for the silver price to go higher. And Wheaton Precious Metals is one of those streamers that pays a dividend too.

Now, these dividends are not quite as high as typical dividends. For comparison, the average dividend paid by the top 500 US companies (the S&P 500) is 1.81%. But Wheaton is pretty close at 1.6%.

And looking at their dividend chart below, they have consistently paid a dividend over the past seven years. Okay, so it's bounced around a bit, but since the price of silver can bounce around too, that's pretty good.

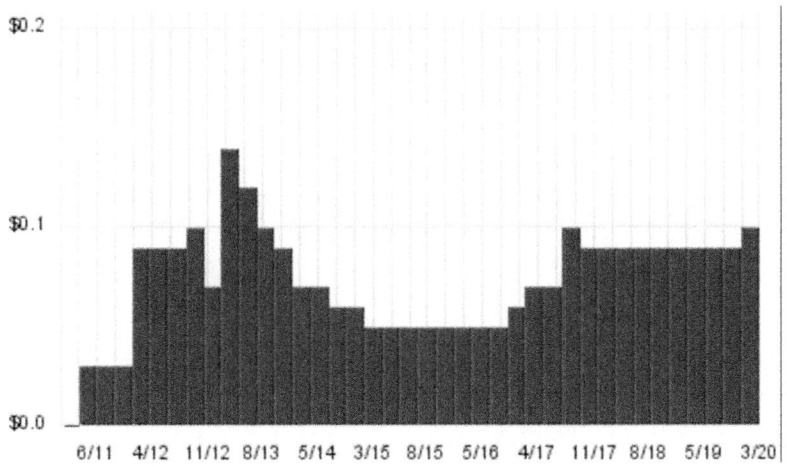

Figure 4-19. Wheaton Precious Metals Dividends
Chart courtesy of DividendChannel.com

So I'd look at the dividend more as an extra bonus, while getting the advantages of exposure to silver in your portfolio.

And at writing, Wheaton Precious Metals has interests in twenty mines. That means there's also the advantage of protection through diversification. So if one mine is disappointing, others may pick up the slack. And they have nine development projects too.

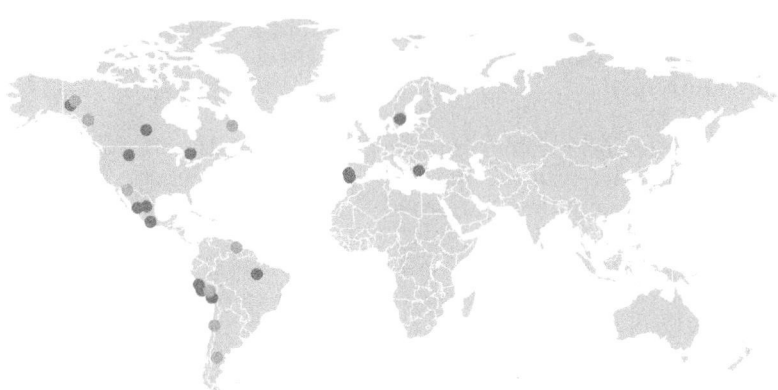

Figure 4-20. Wheaton Precious Metals Diversified Mine Locations
Courtesy of Wheaton Precious Metals - www.Wheatonpm.com

So with all those things in mind, you might want to check out Wheaton Precious Metals (WPM) and see if it fits your unique investment needs and risk tolerance. The company sure seems to have a great business model.

You probably won't be surprised that I've invested in Wheaton throughout the years, and own shares at writing. And I always smile when I think how I'm helping take all of that pesky, bothersome silver off of those poor miner's hands.

I like the streamer / royalty model so well I'm also invested in a couple more. And while they deal in silver streams and royalties, their focus is more on gold and other resources. But the business model is similar, and I don't mind at all that gold is included in the mix.

So here are a couple more streamers for you.

FNV - Franco Nevada

Franco Nevada (FNV), based out of Toronto, Ontario, Canada is one such company. They are a leading gold royalty and streaming company with the largest portfolio of assets. And along with gold, they are very diversified into additional interests in silver, the platinum group, oil, gas and other resources.

Their portfolio includes 340 mineral and gas and oil assets. And these properties are in various stages from early stage exploration through full production.

And they are geographically diverse too, with their investments located in the U.S., Canada, Mexico, Peru, Chile and Africa.

They also pay a dividend at 1.29%, so you are paid to invest in them. And I own shares in them as well.

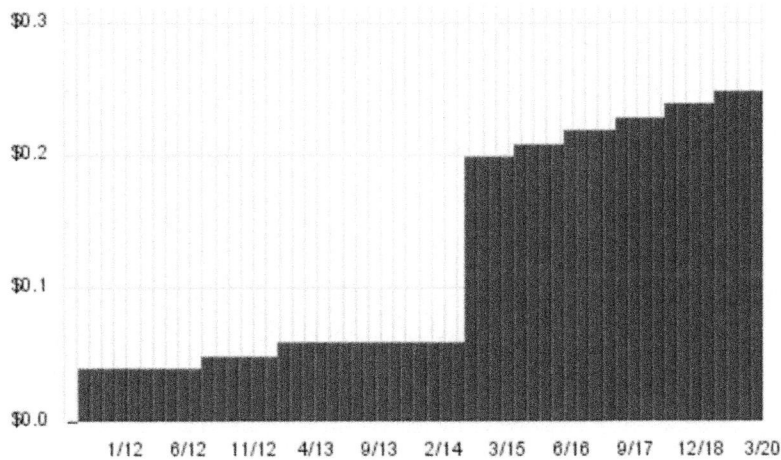

Figure 4-21. Franco Nevada Dividends
Chart courtesy of DividendChannel.com

RGLD - Royal Gold

Royal Gold (RGLD), based out of Denver, Colorado in the US is another streamer and royalty company. And they have claims on gold, silver, copper, lead and zinc mines.

Over half of their developmental properties they have interests in are producing. However, many have not passed the exploration stage.
Their interests are quite diverse in over 20 countries. And most recently they announced the acquisition of a high quality silver stream produced from the Khoemacau Copper Project in Botswana, a country in Southern Africa.

Other properties are located in Canada, Chile, the Dominican Republic, Ghana and Mexico. And they also have stream and royalty interests in mines in Argentina, Australia, Bolivia, Brazil, Burkina Faso, Guatemala, Honduras, Macedonia, Nicaragua, Peru, Russia, Spain and Tunisia.

Royal Gold pays a dividend at 1.15%, so you are paid to invest in them. And they have consistently raised their dividend since 2004, which is pretty impressive for such a risky business as silver mining. So you might guess, correctly, that I also own shares in them at writing.

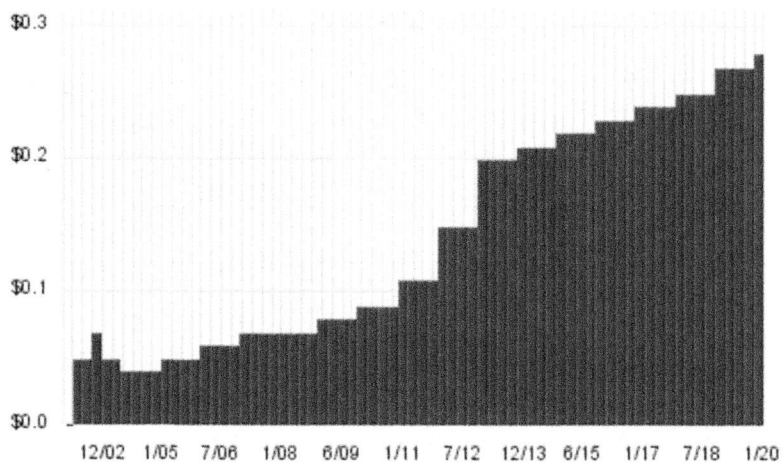

Figure 4-22. Royal Gold Dividends
Chart courtesy of DividendChannel.com

Summary

So those are some streamer and royalty companies for you. They are one of my favorite ways to invest in silver because I like their business model. They offer needed funding to mining companies, and in return, they get a cut of the action.

Also, unusual for precious metals investments, some of them pay you a dividend. And since they have interests in a numerous mines, your risk is spread across them and lowered. In other words, your investment is diversified instead of being concentrated in the fortunes of just one mine or mining company.

That said, there's another way to diversify across numerous silver investments as well. And that is to invest in silver related funds.

Silver Stock Funds

Silver stock funds provide a convenient way to diversify and spread your risk across various silver related companies.

Just think of a fund as a stock with a bunch of other stocks inside of it. And in the case of a silver mining fund, all the stocks inside the fund are silver miners.

Now funds are different than streamers in that they don't have special agreements with the various mining companies. They just own stocks in a number of mining companies, (or other silver related businesses). So when you buy shares of the funds, you are buying a portion of all the silver related businesses they are invested in.

This is much easier for you and I than having to go out and buy shares in each of the individual companies. It's a one-stop shopping thing. So buying shares in funds gets you shares in all those different stocks with one single purchase.

And when the price of silver goes up, all of the reserves of silver mining companies will probably go up in value. So their stock will go up in value. And since your fund owns some of those stocks, your fund will go up in value.

And these funds trade just like stocks. They have a stock symbol just like any other stock you buy and sell on the market. Like the one we're going to look at next called Global X Silver Miners ETF (SIL). It's stock symbol is SIL.

SIL - Global X Silver Miners ETF

The Global X Silver Miners ETF (SIL) is a fund choice that gives you a one-stop buy into a number of global silver miners.

By buying SIL you get instant diversification across over two dozen of them. And these silver producers are fairly diverse geographically as well. About 39% are in to Canada, 18% Mexico, 13% Russia, 12% in the United States, 12% in South Korea, and 6% in Peru.

The fund also pays an annual dividend of 1.26%, which is pretty good for a precious metals investment.

TYPES OF FUNDS: There are many varieties of funds. There at Mutual Funds, Exchange Traded Funds, and Closed End Funds, to name a few. But without getting all hung up in the detailed technicalities of these, we'll just think of them as a basket of stocks under one stock symbol.

My favorites are the Exchange Trades Funds (ETF's) and Closed End Funds (CEF's), because they trade instantly on the stock market just like any stock. The mutual funds require that you wait overnight for your trade (buy or sell) to take effect.

For the more technically inclined, here's a more detailed description of an exchange-traded fund. It's an investment fund traded on stock exchanges, much like stocks. An ETF holds assets such as stocks, commodities, or bonds and generally operates with an arbitrage mechanism designed to keep it trading close to its net asset value, although deviations can occasionally occur.

Or you can just think of it as a basket of stocks under one stock symbol.

Here are the top ten holdings at writing…
- Polymetal International PLC
- **Wheaton Precious Metals Corp**
- Korea Zinc Co Ltd
- **Pan American Silver Corp**
- First Majestic Silver Corp
- SSR Mining Inc
- Fresnillo PLC
- Industrias PeÃ±oles SAB de CV
- Buenaventura Mining Co Inc ADR
- MAG Silver Corp

Note that Wheaton Precious Metals and Pan American Silver, which we discussed earlier, are in the top ten holdings. So you get exposure to these stocks plus over twenty more just by investing in the SIL fund. That's the beauty of funds, and I have invested in SIL off and on in the past for that reason.

SILJ - ETFMG Prime Junior Silver ETF

The ETFMG Prime Junior Silver ETF (SILJ) is similar to the SIL fund, but adds in some of the smaller, more risky miners, known as junior miners. They are engaged in silver refining, mining, or exploration.

Buying this fund gives you a one stop buy into about thirty of these miners. So that's instant diversification for you. These silver producers are not quite as geographically diverse with about 71% in Canada, 2% Latin America, 13% United Kingdom and 14% in the United States.

Unlike SIL, the fund does not pay a dividend, And that is in line with this more speculative investment since it includes some junior miners.

Here are the top ten holdings at writing...
- First Majestic Silver Corp
- Pan American Silver Corp
- Hochschild Mining PLC
- Hecla Mining Co
- MAG Silver Corp
- SSR Mining Inc
- Yamana Gold Inc
- Hudbay Minerals Inc
- Silvercorp Metals Inc
- SilverCrest Metals Inc

Note that there is some overlap in holdings with our previously mentioned SIL fund, such as Pan American Silver. Also, I've not invested in SILJ, although at writing I hold a similar junior miner fund focused on gold (GLDJ).

Silver Tracking And Bullion Funds

We've discussed how funds can own shares of stocks in silver mining companies at this point. And by buying shares of the funds you are getting ownership (indirectly) into shares of the different mining companies.

But shares of a fund don't necessarily have to represent stocks. They can represent other things of value, like actual physical ounces of silver instead. So what if there was a fund where one of their shares represented one ounce of physical silver that they owned? So when the price of silver went up, our shares in the silver fund would go up. And when silver went down, our fund shares would go down.

Our share price would be "tracking" the price of silver, wouldn't it?

And that would be kind of like buying an ounce of silver for each share that we bought in the fund. It would be convenient because we could do this with the click of a mouse. And we wouldn't have to store the silver because storage would be taken care of by the silver fund.

So you won't be surprised when I tell you those types of funds exist. They are known as silver "tracking" funds, and they are convenient to use.

Just note that owning shares in most of these funds does not necessarily mean that you own the silver. Or that you could get access to it in a real financial crisis. Now, some of the funds do allow for delivery of the actual silver on demand, but the minimums are very high. So that rules out taking delivery for most investors, and certainly beginning investors. Also note that not all of the funds are fully backed by silver - they may use other mechanisms to just track the price.

So I would make sure I had bought some real, physical, hold in your hand silver first. Because one of the reasons for holding silver is that it's one of the few financial assets you can own that's outside of the financial system.

But aside from those caveats, many silver investors find silver funds to be a very convenient way to invest in silver. And I've used these types of tracking funds on occasion for short term speculative plays. But not that often, really, since I tend to be more of a long term "investor" in silver stocks and streamers that pay me dividends.

But that said, let's look at some of these silver funds to get the full picture. We'll start with the Aberdeen Standard Physical Silver Shares ETF (SIVR).

SIVR Aberdeen Standard Physical Silver Shares ETF
The Aberdeen Physical Silver ETF fund holds physical silver and issues shares. As they say, the fund is designed for investors who want a cost effective and convenient way to invest in silver. And the objective is that the shares reflect the price of silver (less the trust's expenses).

You can buy and sell shares of this fund in your stock trading account using the stock symbol SIVR. So it's very convenient to get in and out of. And its price rises and falls as the demand for silver rises and falls.

At writing the price of a share is $14.36. That represents about an ounce of silver. And the Aberdeen Standard Physical Silver Shares ETF has 21,745,411 ounces of silver valued at around 325,295,275.

They say on their web site that their fund is physically backed with allocated metal. Also, that it's inspected twice per year by Inspectorate International. One of these inspections is also stated to be random. And the vault location where the silver is stored is in London, England.

Since SIVR essentially represents a pile of silver, it does not pay a dividend. And while I don't own it at writing, it's something I would consider investing in. That's because they own the physical silver to back the fund.

Buying shares of SIVR carries the normal risk of the price of silver going down, similar to physical ownership. You can visit their site at https://www.aberdeenstandardetfs.us/institutional/us/en-us/products/product/etfs-physical-silver-shares-sivr-arca. Or just Google "Aberdeen Standard Silver Shares ETF SIVR."

PSLV Sprott Physical Silver Trust

Sprott Physical Silver Trust (PSLV) holds physical silver at a secure third-party location. So this fund also lets investors get the benefit of owning physical silver, but without the drawback of having to store it and keep it in good condition.

The price of PSLV also rises and falls with the demand for silver. At writing, the price of a share is $5.56, so that represents about 1/3 of an ounce of silver (.374 oz) per share. And the Sprott Physical Silver Trust has 55,815,375 ounces of silver valued at $829,667,647 at writing.

Sprott says on their web site that "without exception, all of the bullion owned by the Trusts is held in the Trusts' allocated accounts in physical form." And since PSLV essentially represents a pile of silver, it does not pay a dividend.

I currently don't own PSLV, although it's something I would consider investing in. That's because they own the physical silver to back the fund. Buying shares of PSLV carries the normal risk of the price of silver going up or down, similar to physical ownership.

You can visit their site at http://sprott.com/investment-strategies/physical-bullion-trusts/why-consider-sprott-trusts/. Or just Google "Sprott Physical Silver Trust PSLV."

SLV - iShares Silver Trust

The iShares Silver Trust (SLV) is another Exchange Traded Fund (ETF) that seeks to generally reflect the performance of the price of silver. Like the other ETF's, it's an easy way to gain exposure to silver without worrying about buying and storing the physical metal.

SLV is also the largest fund in its segment. It began trading in April, 2006 and tracks the silver spot price, less expenses and liabilities, using silver bullion held in vaults in London. At writing, SLV currently has about $4.8 billion in net assets including 319,819,396 ounces in the Trust. You can check out SLV at the web sites https://www.etf.com/SLV or https://www.ishares.com/us/products/239855/ishares-silver-trust-fund.

The fund expense ratio is significantly higher than comparable funds. So it will cost you more to own it. That said, what I like about SLV is that it's the most liquid fund in its peer group. i.e. there are many buyers and sellers. Which means it trades easily for retail and institutional investors alike.

Also, I like the fact that a share of SLV is about the same price as an ounce of silver, although it doesn't track exactly. For example, at writing, a share of SLV was $15.52 and the spot price for silver was $16.58. So that's tracking the silver price pretty well.

Since SLV essentially represents a pile of silver, it does not pay a dividend. I've owned SLV off and on in the past, usually for shorter term speculation trades, but do not own it at writing.

Buying shares of SLV carries the normal risk of the price of silver going up or down, similar to physical ownership. But remember that owning SLV isn't necessarily the same as owning physical silver. Also, taking delivery of physical silver bullion is pretty much out of reach for most investors, since one must deal in 50,000 share blocks.

And since you don't have the physical silver with you, there is always the risk that funds do not have all of the silver. This is known as counter party risk, i.e. you are trusting another party to have what they say they do.

Finally, in a severe economic or geopolitical crises, the shares may not be exchangeable like physical silver would be.

That said, for many situations, SLV may work just fine. It's easy to invest in, and has a low entry point for beginning investors, i.e. you can buy as little as one share in your stock trading account.

~~~~~

So we've looked at three silver tracking funds at this point. Their objective is to mimic owning silver by tracking its price. But tracking funds can have objectives other than that.

For example, what if there was a fund that went up (or down) TWICE AS FAST as the price of silver. And sure enough, funds like that exist. Which leads us to the ProShares 2X Ultra Silver (AGQ).

AGQ - ProShares 2X Ultra Silver

The ProShares Ultra Silver Trust (AGQ) began trading on 12/01/2008 and is an ETF that tries to match the price of silver at *two times* the rate, instead of just tracking one for one like the other silver ETF's we just looked at. So if you are really gung ho on silver in the short term, and think it is going to rise, you can supercharge you investment by buying AGQ. Because if the silver price goes up, your silver fund will go up about twice as much.

The ProShares Ultra Silver Trust uses futures and options to get this leverage. So this is a pretty speculative play with more risk. It's share price rises faster, and falls faster, than the price of silver. So this is not for the weak of heart.

Also, this should be a short term play as the double tracking is for just one day. Then it can begin to drift. Or as they say, the ETF seeks a return that is 2x the return of its underlying benchmark (target) *for a single day*.

SLV and OPTIONS: I do an occasional silver options trade and often use options on SLV to do that. Technically speaking, that's because SLV gives me many choices, i.e. it has very deep options chains (strike prices) and many speculators (open interest). Or to put it more simply, buying and selling is easy, as there are many players to buy from and sell to.

But note that options and futures are definitely not recommended for beginning investors, as they require a lot of attention and a higher skill level. They can be very volatile, and while traders can make a lot of money fast, they can also lose a lot of money fast. And beginners often lose.

Due to the compounding of daily returns, the returns over periods other than one day will likely differ in amount and possibly direction from the target return for the same period. So you would want to monitor your holdings at least daily.

So this is not a particularly good investment beginning investors should make. Or as one description puts it, "Not suitable for all investors, these ETFs or other exchange traded products represent unique risks, including leverage, derivatives, and complex investment strategies." I have simply included it so you can see the range of investment products out there for silver.

But here's a real life example of how it works. Back in June 20, 2019, the markets got nervous as Iran shot down a United States drone in the Straits of Hormuz area. SLV jumped from $14 to $14.50 for an increase of $.50 a share. That same day, AGQ jumped from $24 to $25 for a double increase of $1.00 per share. Actually, it went a bit higher for part of the day.

So that's an example of how a two times (2X) fund works. And you can check it out at this web site address - https://research.ameritrade.com/grid/wwws/etfs/profile/charts.asp?symbol=AGQ. Or Google search "AGQ ProShares 2X Ultra Silver."

Now if you really want to get crazy, there's a fund that tries to get **three times** the move on silver (technically, the daily performance of the silver index - S&P GSCI Silver Index ER). The fund is called the ProShares 3X Ultra Silver (USLV). I don't believe I've ever used a 3X fund, and only used a 2X fund a few times.

OK, so we've really gotten out in left field at this point with that 3X fund. But I'll give you one more tricky fund here, and then we'll return to the world of sanity.

So here it is. Believe it or not, there's a fund that tries to move double, but backwards, to the price of silver. Maybe we would call it the -2X fund. In other words, if the price of silver goes DOWN $1, this fund goes UP $2. So why would anyone want something like that? To learn more, read on.

ZSL ProShares -2X UltraShort Silver Fund

Up to this point, as we've talked about tracking funds, we've had an assumption going on in the back of our minds. And that is that when silver goes up, the tracking fund shares go up, and we make money.

And that's pretty much how they work. So by buying these funds, we are betting that the price of silver is going up.

But the price of silver doesn't always go up. Sometimes it goes down. So what if we thought the price of silver was going down in the near future. Is there a way we could make money?

And the answer is yes. The ProShares 2X UltraShort Silver Trust (ZSL) shares INCREASE in value when the price of silver GOES DOWN. They track the price of silver in reverse. So if you thought the price of silver was going down, you could buy ZSL. And its price would move up (approximately) at **two times** the price drop of silver, because it's a 2X tracking fund.

Here's how ProShares describes it... "ProShares UltraShort Silver seeks daily investment results, before fees and expenses, that correspond to two times the inverse (-2x) of the daily performance the Bloomberg Silver SubindexSM."

So how do they do this? Well, without getting too technical, they use a technique like selling short, which is a way to make money when an investment is going down in price instead of up. By the way, you can sell regular stocks short too, if you think their price is going down.

All the caveats for ProShares Ultra Silver Trust apply to ZSL. That is, they use futures and options to get this leverage. So this is also a pretty speculative play and there is more risk. Remember, prices rise faster, and fall faster with this ETF as well - again, not for the weak of heart.

By the way, note that they also say, "This fund is not an investment company regulated under the Investment Company Act of 1940 and is not afforded its protections." So be forewarned.

Also, this should be a short term play, as the double tracking is for one day and then it could begin to drift. Or as they say, the ETF seeks a return that is two times the inverse (-2x) of the return of its underlying benchmark (target) *for a single day.*

Due to the compounding of daily returns, the returns over periods other than one day may begin to drift in amount and possibly direction from the target return for the same period. So you should monitor your holdings as frequently as daily.

All that said, this is not an investment that most beginning investors will be making. But it does show you the variety of funds out there. And I think it's good to be aware of them, and how people can use them to make money even when the price of silver drops.

Futures And Options

Futures and options are not for beginning investors, but we'll just touch on them to give you the overall picture. They involve entering into contracts to buy or sell specified amounts of silver or silver related securities at a specified price by a specified date.

For example, a futures contract might specify to buy 5000 ounces of silver for $20 an ounce by November 14, 2019. Just to get your attention, if you had not gotten out of that contract by November 14, 2019, you would be on the hook for a $100,000 to purchase that silver.

These highly leveraged plays allow you to achieve bigger profits (or losses) by controlling larger amounts of silver than if you made an outright purchase. However, they carry substantial risk, are much more complex than a stock investment, and require expertise.

Also, you must pay close attention to them. They're not like stocks where you can just check up on them every once and a while. That's because prices can move quickly and futures and options have an expiration date (like our example above).

You also need a special commodities account to do futures, which trade in totally different exchange(s) than your stock investing account. Or you can trade options on Silver ETFs and silver stocks in your stock investing account. But like above, they also have an expiration date. So if the market doesn't go your way, and you let them expire, you lose the money you paid for them. And if you sold some that didn't go your way, you are forced to buy shares for more than you sold the options for.

I have traded some options on silver futures in the past in a commodities account. I don't recommend it and it's not for the faint of heart. I also do an occasional option play on silver ETFs in one of my stock investing accounts. The ETF I prefer for this is SLV because it is so widely traded.

But I don't recommend this for beginning investors either. So unless you are going to put in some serious study to learn about futures and options, and I mean weeks, months or years, depending on your level of effort, beginning investors should stay away from these trades.

Because you can achieve your silver investing goals by outright purchase of physical silver, and silver stocks and funds, with much less complexity and risk. So let's look into these simpler ways to invest right now.

5

HOW TO BUY SILVER

There are any number of ways you can buy (and sell) silver. Here are three of them that I like and use...

- Visit a local coin dealer and buy physical silver.
- Buy physical silver online.
- Buy silver stocks and funds through your stock account if you have one.

You may find some or all of these useful, so let's have a look at them all.

Buy From Your Local Coin Dealer

Buying from your local coin dealer is a great way to buy silver and has a number of advantages. These include no shipping cost, instant gratification, and anonymity. So this has been one of my favorite ways to buy physical, hold in your hand silver. And it's how I first got started.

As it turns out, a coin dealer is located not too far from where I grocery shop here in Orlando. So in the past, when I bought groceries, I'd often add a visit to his coin shop and buy a few ounces of silver for cash.

This was something I enjoyed, and through repeated visits, I got to know Jason, the coin shop owner. And he got to know me as a customer, and that I typically bought US Silver Eagles. So when I showed up at his shop, he would buzz me in the front door and say "hello and how many?" I'd say something like, "Five silver Eagles this time." Then he'd give me the coins, I'd give him the cash, and I'd be on my way. It was as simple as that.

By the way, one of the nice things about buying from a local dealer with cash is the privacy benefit. As long as you don't buy too much silver at one time ($10,000), the transaction is completely anonymous and private.

Other times, if he wasn't too busy, we would talk for a while about silver and the decline of the dollar. And often I would say how I felt bad that I was giving him those worthless paper dollars, and he was giving me pure silver coins in return. It became kind of a standing joke between us.

And sometimes I enjoyed looking at all of the different silver products he had on display. This is something you might enjoy too, and is a nice feature of buying from your local coin dealer. It's fun to look at their showcases filled with the different coins, bars and rounds. Some of them are quite striking.

But don't get carried away here. Stay the course and stick to your plan when you actually buy something. Remember, you are there strictly to buy the silver for its bullion value, not the numismatic (scarcity) value of the coins.

You're not there as a coin collector (unless that's your thing). So when you visit a local coin dealer the first time, tell him "you want to buy silver coins strictly for their bullion value, not their numismatic value," and he'll know what you mean.

Numismatic Value vs. Silver Bullion Value: There are two parts of a coins price: The value of the silver it contains and it's numismatic value. Numismatic value is determined by the scarcity, or how rare it is, and the coin's condition. In other words, it's collectors value.

To use an extreme example, a Morgan Silver dollar minted in 1893 in the San Francisco mint is very rare. It might cost $9500. But it only has .77 of an ounce of silver which is worth $15.40 if silver is $20 per ounce. So the numismatic value is $9484.60 and the silver bullion value is $15.40.

By the way, numismatic is pronounced noo-miz-mat'-ik.

Another advantage of buying from your local dealer is there's no shipping charge. Because when you leave, you have the silver in hand. And even better, it's an instant gratification thing, and what's not to like about that.

Now, coin dealers have to eat, so understand you will have to pay a premium for the coins you buy. And that premium may vary depending on if the demand for the coins is heavy or light.

To give you an example, some years ago when silver was at $17 an ounce, I would pay $20 for one ounce US Silver Eagles, or $19 for Canadian Silver Maple Leafs. But on rare occasion, I might have to pay an extra dollar or two more for the Eagles, as demand for them increased and the dealer had trouble getting them. So be aware that premiums can vary from time to time.

That said, buying from your local coin dealer is a good way to get started. And it's pretty simple to find them. Just go to Google and type in "Coin Dealers in *your city*." For example, I typed in "Coin Dealers in Orlando" when I was looking.

Then pick one nearest to where you live, or work, and give them a call or a visit. Depending on what you want to buy, ask them if they sell 1) one ounce US Silver Eagles or 2) Canadian Maple Leafs and/or 3) loose junk silver coins like pre-1965 silver dimes, etc. A yes to most questions is a good sign.

You should also look up their Better Business Bureau rating. You can do this by going to a search engine like Google and searching for "*silver dealer name* Better Business Bureau profile." And look for a pattern of problems. And if they have a web site, you should look at their customer comments too.

But if all of this checks out, then you may have just found your local coin dealer. Now go pay them a visit. I think you'll find the experience to be fun and rewarding as you become familiar with their silver products and prices.

And holding your first one ounce .999 pure silver coin is pretty exciting. Because they are beautiful, and the heft of them in your hand just feels like something of value.

So this is a great way to get started. Then once you've started building your stack of silver, you can move on to other silver investments if you like. But most people should start here with physical silver first.

Buy Online

Another good way to buy silver bullion is online. What I like about buying online is how fast and easy it is - particularly once you've identified a reputable online dealer and made a purchase. At that point, future purchases are just a few mouse clicks away.

I'll give you the names of a couple of online dealers that I use. Or you can look for a dealer by doing a Google search for "buy silver online." This will get you many choices offering silver bullion bars and coins.

But note that you need to use as much caution or more checking out online dealers as you do with local dealers. One way to do this is to check the Better Business Bureau to see how they rate. As before, you can do this by going to a search engine like Google and searching for "*silver dealer name* Better Business Bureau profile."

When you go to the profile it will tell you a number of things. To me, the most important is the BBB (Better Business Bureau) rating. Also, it will tell you if they are accredited and give you access to Customer Reviews and Customer complaints. And look for a pattern of problems, especially slow deliveries.

A company that constantly has trouble making prompt deliveries may be close to insolvent. Also, there should be a reasonable explanation for delivery delays. And if they have a web site, you should look at their customer comments too.

So be sure and do this step and look the information over. Here's why.

Some years back I made a purchase from an online dealer. And my order was delivered and the service was satisfactory. But as I look them up in the Better Business Bureau today, they are listed as not accredited, they have a rating of B and some customer complaints.

I try not to buy from anyone rated less than A. Also, further research shows they had a lawsuit around March of 2016. So I don't buy from them today.

Now compare that to when I search on my local coin dealer. He is accredited, has a rating of A+, five star customer reviews, and no complaints. This squares with my experience as a customer. His service and quality is great. So of course, I keep buying from him.

So be sure and do your due diligence before you buy. It only takes a few minutes to look up an online dealer. And it can help you avoid some problems.

So all that said, here are a couple of online dealers that I use.

JM Bullion

JM Bullion, a precious metals products retailer, provides a convenient, straight forward way to buy your silver online. Established in 2011, they are located in Dallas, Texas in the US. They deal exclusively in physical bullion, selling silver (and gold, platinum,, etc.) that is delivered directly to your door.

They have a very wide variety of products to choose from. They have US Silver Eagles and Canadian Maple Leafs as well as many other sovereign coins. They also have junk silver coins, bars, rounds, and yes, even silver bullets. In short, they have virtually every physical silver product mentioned in this book. And their minimum purchase is quite low, so that's good for beginning investors on a budget. I actually put this to the test in the past by ordering, and receiving, just two US silver eagles (and I could have ordered just one, but wanted to spread the shipping cost a bit).
Their delivery was quite fast. I placed the order online on a Monday, and received it just three days later, in my mailbox, that Thursday. That's pretty good, especially when you consider there was a holiday (New Year's) within that three day span.
Their website and order process is also easy to understand and use. And you can buy from them without an account, or you can set up an account, which is easy to do too.
At writing, they have an A+ rating with the Better Business Bureau and have been an Accredited Business since 7/14/2014. And they also have five star customer reviews.
So if you just can't get yourself out of the easy chair, and the convenience of online purchasing interest you, their site is worth a visit. You can check them out at www.jmbullion.com.

Please note that I have no affiliation with JM Bullion aside from being a satisfied customer. Also, always do your own due diligence to check them out, as situations can change over time.

OWNX.com

OWNx.com is a precious metals custodial dealer based in Lawrence, Kansas in the US. They are my favorite online dealer because of their automatic purchase program.

Another feature of OWNx that I like is that you can store your precious metals in OWNx's vault - hence the term "custodial dealer." And their premium and storage fees are quite reasonable, so that's what I do. I let them worry about keeping my silver safe.

Or you can take delivery once you've accumulated at least 20 ounces of silver or 1 ounce of gold. Once you've hit that threshold, you can have your precious metals delivered to your house if you like. And you have a choice of what you would like delivered.

For silver, you can get one ounce coins (I prefer US Silver Eagles) or silver bars (1, 10 100 or even 1000 ounce - wow). Or you can get silver rounds as well. And for gold you can get one ounce coins or kilo bars.

OWNx can handle small and large investors, so they are a good site for beginning investors. Their minimum purchase is $25 to get started. So you can start small and buy in fractional ounces (silver) and grains (gold). But to show their full range, you can make over $100,000 purchases as well.

At writing, they are Better Business Bureau accredited, have an A+ rating, five star customer reviews, and showed no customer complaints.

As I mentioned earlier, what really sets them apart for me is their automatic purchase program. With this program you can set up a fixed dollar amount for automatic withdrawal from your checking account (shows on your bank statement as "Electronic Withdrawal Mass Metal LLC").

And you can have it automatically purchase silver with those funds and have it stored in your silver account. So this is "set it and forget it," silver buying.

So if this kind of automatic purchasing interest you, their site is worth a visit. I find their web site and screens to be pretty straight forward and easy to use. And you can check them out right here at www.OWNx.com.
 Please note that at writing I have no interest or affiliation with OWNx aside from being a satisfied customer. Also, always do your own due diligence checking them out, as situations can change over time.

Buy In Your Stock Account

For those who want to go beyond buying physical silver, you can also invest in silver related stocks and funds using your stock market account. Like other online buying, it's convenient and as quick as a mouse click.

And it's another one of my favorite ways to invest in silver. That's because you can see the instant effect in your account as the price of silver goes up or down. So that's pretty direct feedback. Also, as we mentioned earlier, some silver stocks and funds can have bigger price movements than the underlying silver price. So that can mean faster and bigger profits (just be mindful that prices can go faster and bigger in the down direction as well).

Now, when you're investing through your stock account, you're typically not buying silver outright, or taking physical delivery. Rather, as we discussed in the previous chapter, you're buying silver mining stocks, silver streamers, silver stock funds / ETF's, or silver tracking and bullion funds.

Buying these stocks and funds is as simple as buying any other stocks and funds. You just place an order using their unique stock symbol, like any other stock or fund.

For example, let's say you want to buy 10 shares of the iShares Silver Trust ETF (SLV) that we looked in the previous chapter. Its stock symbol is SLV. And let's say you are willing to pay the current asking price of $16.88 a share that you see when you look it up.

Then you will enter your order into a screen that looks something like this...

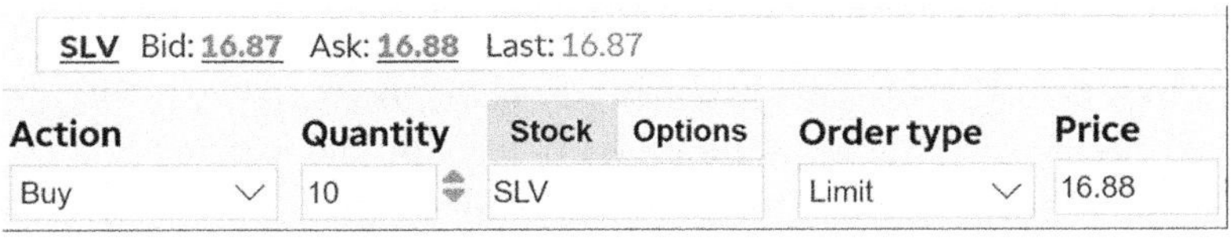

SLV Bid: **16.87** Ask: **16.88** Last: 16.87				
Action	**Quantity**	**Stock** Options	**Order type**	**Price**
Buy ⌄	10 ⇕	SLV	Limit ⌄	16.88

Figure 5-1. Stock Account Order Screen

After you review your order and hit the place order button (not shown), within seconds your order will get filled (typically) and you now own 10 shares of SLV in your stock trading account.

It's about that simple and quick.

I really like investing in silver related stock and fund investments. At writing, I own a number of them, including three of my favorites listed below...

- Wheaton Precious Metals (WPM) - 1.4% Dividend
- Franco Nevada Corp Com (FNV) - 1.0% Dividend
- Royal Gold Inc Com (RGLD) - 1.1% Dividend

We discussed these three stocks earlier in this chapter and I've owned all three for some time. Also note that I chose them because they all pay a dividend, which is somewhat unusual for precious metals investments. But then, I like to get paid to invest.

So all that said, for those who want to go beyond buying physical silver, investing in silver related stocks and funds using your stock market account can be a good way to go.

Buying Strategies And Techniques

Okay, at this point we know we can invest in silver a number of ways. We can go visit our local coin dealer. Or we can buy online. Or we can buy shares of stocks and funds in our stock trading account.

But how we do all of this in a way that we buy intelligently, at the best price, or in amounts that we can afford? Because most of us cannot just go out and buy all the silver we think we need in a one and done transaction.

Well, here are some practical approaches and techniques that I use. And we'll start off with one of my favorites, which I think you're going to like. By the way, it's a favorite of legendary investor Warren Buffett too.

For those who do not understand stock investing and/or don't have a stock account, you may be interested in my book ***Stock Investing For Beginners***. It covers the basics including setting up an account and walking you through the buying and selling process step by step. You can check it out right here or for those with a print book, at www.amazon.com ***Stock Investing For Beginners*** by John Roberts. It is simple to understand and has over 500 positive reader reviews..

It's called dollar cost averaging and it makes a financial genius out of you. And it's very easy to do.

Dollar Cost Averaging

One good strategy is to buy a little bit of silver at a time. This works well for many beginning investors because it takes less money up front. You just slowly accumulate silver and build your position over time.

To use a concrete example, let's assume you want to buy the US Silver Eagle one ounce coins. And let's say you have about $60 per month to invest, and Eagles are going for $20 each at the moment.

Now, there are two ways you can do this. One way is to buy three coins every month. And that's not too bad, actually. But there's a much better way.

And that is to buy $60 worth of Eagles every month. In other words, buy the **same dollar amount** of silver each time instead of the same number of coins. Because that makes a difference.

You can see the two methods side by side in the table below. In the **3 Eagles Per Month - GOOD** table on the left, you are buying three Silver Eagles every month regardless of the price. So when the price is high you are buying as many Eagles as when the price is low.

For example, in Month 2 the price was really high at $30 a coin, and you still bought three coins, even at that high price. Then in Month 3 the price dropped in half to $15 a coin, but you still only bought three coins. You didn't take advantage of the cheaper price.

| | 3 Eagles Per Month - GOOD | | | | | $60 Per Month - BETTER! | | | | |
| | A | B | C | D | E | F | G | H | I | J |
	Buy 3 Silver Eagles Per Month	Price Per Coin	Number of Coins	Total Paid	Average Price Per Coin (Ounce)	Buy $60 of Silver Eagles Per Month	Price Per Coin	Number of Coins	Total Paid	Average Price Per Coin (Ounce)
Month 1	3	$20	3	$60	$20.00	$60	$20	3	$60	$20.00
Month 2	3	$30	3	$90	$30.00	$60	$30	2	$60	$30.00
Month 3	3	$15	3	$45	$15.00	$60	$15	4	$60	$15.00
Total			9	$195	$21.67			9	$180	$20.00

Figure 5-2. Dollar Cost Averaging Advantage

But it would be better to buy less Eagles when the price is high, and more when the price is low. And an easy, dead simple way to do this is to just buy $60 worth of Eagles every month. You can see this illustrated in the **$60 Per Month - BETTER** example in the right hand of the table.

So the first month, Eagles are going for $20, so you buy three of them. But the second month, they are expensive at $30, so you only buy two of them. Then the third month they are cheap at $15, so you buy four of them. By following you $60 per month rule, you are automatically buying more when the price is low, and less when the price is high.

And just look at the results. In both cases, you wound up with 9 Eagles. But your average cost in the first example is $21.67 per Eagle. In the second example, it's only $20 per Eagle. That's much better, yes?

So by setting a specific **dollar cost** to spend, your **average** cost per Eagle is less. Which is why buying like this is called **"dollar cost averaging."** So for less money and no effort, you got the same amount of Eagles. You're a financial genius!

Now, realistically, the price of silver, and Eagles, probably won't bounce around that much month to month. I just used those numbers to illustrate the point. And some months, buying a fixed dollar amount would require you to try to buy a fraction of a coin, which you can't really do.

For example, if the Eagle price was $24 when you went to buy your $60 worth of silver, you would want to buy 2.5 eagles ($60 / $24 = 2.5 eagles). Now, you can't really buy 2.5 eagle coins.

So what you can do is round up the fraction .5 or more to the next whole number of coins - in this case 3 eagles. Or if your fraction was .4 or below, round down to 2 eagles. And over time your rounding should even out to dollar cost averaging.

So that's how you can dollar cost average when buying individual coins.

But it's even easier if you are buying from an online dealer like OWNx, discussed earlier. Because they will actually let you buy, and carry your account balance, in fractions of an ounce of silver. So you can easily execute dollar cost averaging with them - no rounding required.

And using our example above, you can set the whole thing up to buy $60 a month automatically, so you never even have to think about it. It just happens - as the most efficient possible way for you to buy.

Another advantage of dollar cost averaging that I really appreciate is psychological. Because when prices move down against you, it eases some of the sting. That's because you can view the downturn as an improved buying opportunity, rather than a disappointing loss.

So this is a great way to buy silver and take advantage of its price swings. I do it all of the time, and you might want to do so as well.

And that leads us to another strategy I like, that works well when buying silver related stocks and funds. It helps you buy at amazing discounts. Now hang on, because it's called the Stink Bid Strategy (or Low-Ball Order if that's to colorful for you).

Sounds kind of dramatic, doesn't it? And it can be a bit "iffy" too. But you'd be surprised at how often it actually works.

The Stink Bid Strategy

This strategy works best when you are buying silver stocks or funds in your stock account. And what's great about it is it costs you nothing to set it up. Now note that this doesn't always work, but when it does, you can get silver stocks and funds at a nice discount.

Now remember, when you are buying a silver stock or fund in your trading account, what you are really doing is placing an order. And that order goes out to the stock exchange. And some buyer, somewhere in the world, sees that order on the stock exchange, and if the price is right, they sell you the stock (or fund - we'll just say stock from now on).

In other words, your order gets filled, usually in seconds, and you own the stock. So overall, that's how buying a stock really happens, i.e. place an order, order gets filled.

Now there are two different kinds of orders you can place.

One order is to buy the stock at whatever everyone else is paying for it at the moment. Or put another way, you just want to buy the shares at the **market** price. This is called a **"market order."**

Basically you are saying, "Hey, I just want to buy these shares at whatever price they cost right now." And typically, your order will get filled quickly at whatever price that is. And usually, the price is okay.

But a better way to buy is to use another kind of order, called a **"limit order."** In this kind of order you are very specific about the highest price you will pay. It's like you said, "I want to buy 100 shares of Wheaton Precious Metals stock at no more than $20 a share." In other words, you **limited** the price of the order to $20 or less per share.

This is the best way to do things because it keeps you in control of the maximum you pay for a stock. Otherwise, if you use a market order, which is kind of a blank check and like saying, "Hey, I'll pay whatever," you could get a rude surprise with a higher price than you expected.

So I always place limit orders. If I really want to buy the stock right now, I just look at what the current market price is, and consider that my limit. Then I place a limit order for that amount. And the order usually gets filled.

If not, and I really want to buy the stock now, I might jigger the limit price up a few cents and replace the limit order with that higher limit order. And keep doing this until it gets filled - assuming I don't have to move it up too high to where it's not a good buy.

But usually I'm not so impatient. After all, what's the hurry? Stock prices go up and stock prices go down. And I know it's really important to get a good price.

And with a limit order, I can specify how long I want the order to remain open. For example, I can say I will pay $20 for WPM anytime it gets to that price in the next three months. So if WPM is selling pretty close to $20 a share right now, if I'm just patient and leave the order out there, I'll probably get the order filled eventually.

As a matter of fact, why not push this idea and try to get the stock cheaper?

For example, let's say its July 1 and you want to buy Wheaton Precious Metals (WPM -one of my favorite silver streamers) and the current price per share is $20. But instead of buying at that price, you put in a limit order for $17 a share. And you make your order good 'til canceled on September 30. In other words, your order is open for the next three months.

Sounds kind of crazy, doesn't it. Who on earth is going to sell you those shares for $17 a share?

But you're patient and just let the order sit out there. And sure enough, the silver market drops and WPM stock goes to $17 a share just one month later on August 1. And your order gets filled at that ridiculously cheap price.

Then over the next 12 months, the price of silver starts rising until your shares are worth $28 per share. And you've made an extra $3 profit because you bought at $17 instead of $20 a share. Nice. And that's the real power of these low ball limit orders. They make it easy to wait for a discounted price to come to you.

And you can get really crazy with this idea too. Believe it or not, I have put in a few orders at a 30-40% discount - AND HAD THEM EVENTUALLY FILLED!.

Now this won't happen very often. But it happens enough that professionals often use this technique. There's even a name for these low ball orders. Like we said, they're called "stink bids." Because they are so low that you can just imagine a seller looking at them and saying, "God, these bids really stink!"

But the seller's opinion aside, sometimes one of them goes ahead and sells, and the low ball order really does get filled. And that's good for you. Especially when you know that setting up these orders cost you nothing to do. So you really have nothing to lose.

And interestingly, the stocks I've bought like this are typically natural resource stocks like gold or silver companies, or small oil companies. Because these stocks can fluctuate like crazy sometimes.

Now the odds of these extreme bids working out are somewhat low. And you will probably be buying most of your stocks at a more normal price, or a small discount. But hey, there's no harm in trying for a few days.
 And I use these low bid orders for another reason as well. Sometimes, if I'm enthused about three or four good stocks, but don't want to invest in all of them, I'll put in stink bids for all of them with an expiration date of 6-8 months out. So these bids kind of serve as a stock reminder for me, like an electronic buy list.

And they just sit out there.

And every once in a while, a price miracle happens and one of the orders fills. And I'm always surprised - pleasantly, I might add. So you might try a low ball order sometime. And you might be surprised as well.

But if you want a dead certain way to build your silver investment over time, here's one that always works. I call it the Alchemist Coffee Can Trick, and anybody can do it.

The Alchemist Coffee Can Trick

Figure 5-3. Convert Base Metal Coins To Silver And Gold

Here's a little trick I do to painlessly accumulate more silver. And every time I do it, I feel like one of the Alchemist of old in 12th century Europe.

You remember them, right? They were the guys with the funny pointed hats that would use various chemicals, elements, incantations and other questionable mumbo jumbo to try to turn base metals into gold. As you can guess, their processes didn't work out so well.

But I do my own modern alchemist trick to turn base metals into silver. And my process works every time.

Because each evening I take my pocket change and throw it into an old 11 ounce Folgers coffee can. And after 4-5 months the can is full of change. So that's my base metal, because our coins no longer contain silver like they did before 1965. They're made out of mostly copper, with a little nickel.

Then once my coffee can is full, I take it to my local grocery store and empty it into a coin counting machine. The machine sorts and counts the coins in about a minute, and prints out a receipt for about $100. Then I take the receipt to the grocery store clerk and they give me $100 in cash.

I take that $100 cash to my nearby coin shop and buy five one-ounce .999 pure US Silver Eagles with it. So now I've transformed my cheap base metal coins into pure silver.

That's some trick for an alchemist, right? And it works every time. And it's all perfectly legal to do this too, although it's such a good deal that it kind of feels like I'm stealing something.

Now, you can do better than me with this technique, as I'm not particularly efficient with it. That's because the coin counting machine deducts 8% from the total as a charge for counting the coins.

So if you want to count the coins and roll them yourself, and trade them for cash at the bank, you can duck that charge and get more money to buy silver. Or maybe you can get the bank to count them for you and make a deposit into your account.

Just please don't show up at your coin dealers with a can full of coins and expect them to count them for you. Go get the cash first.

But isn't that a neat little trick to accumulate some more pure physical silver in your portfolio? So the next time you come home from work or shopping, just throw your pocket change into a container. And that's the start to your silver fund, right there.

Also note you can use a coffee can from a different brand of coffee besides Folgers and the technique should still work just fine - chuckle. And no alchemist incantations or pointy hat required.

A Little Respect For The Alchemists: OK, while I'm poking a little fun at the ancient alchemist, many of our most revered scientists dabbled in alchemy, including Sir Isaac Newton. And they did make some useful scientific discoveries. So in terms of history, and to show a little respect, we'll recognize that the alchemists were the scientists of their time.

When To Sell

When to sell is one of the more difficult questions when speculating and investing. But we'll start off with some simple clues that will be hard to miss.

For example, when you see people forming long lines to cash in their silver at local coin and pawn shops. And ladies are selling their silver tea sets, families hocking their silverware and coin collectors cashing in their collections.

Or when you hear that SLV, the silver Exchange Traded Fund, is being discussed on the Financial TV shows. Or the dramatic rise in silver is in the news on CNN.

Or when your friends, who never gave silver a second thought, are bragging about buying Wheaton Precious Metals (WPM) or Pan American Silver (PAAS) at a cocktail party.

Or when you walk into your local bank and see they have displays on the floor with bars of silver and gold that you can buy.

Then that's the time to sell some of your silver.

Does the scenario I just described have a familiar sound to it? I'll bet it does, because it's how we started this book when we described what was going on in 1979 - 1980.

That was when the price of silver had gone from $6 to $50 an ounce. And things like that really happened, including the silver and gold displays in bank lobbies. I know, because I distinctly remember seeing these as a young man.

Another time you might have sold some silver was in April of 2011 when the market got spooked and approached $50 an ounce - again.

So booms in silver do happen from time to time.

Now the flip side of this is when silver goes down. For those owning physical silver, many will probably just hang on, or buy more. That's easier to do when you have the physical silver. You can just hang on to it for better times. After all, your physical silver is partly an insurance policy you keep against a future financial disaster.

But for those invested in silver stocks and funds, they may want to set a limit on how low they can go down before they **stop** the **loss** and sell them. These selling limits are actually called **stop losses**, and we use them with other stocks or funds that we own as well. For example, a typical stop loss might be to sell when we have lost 25% from our stock purchase price. And we'll cover these in more detail in a later chapter on protecting your silver investment.

So at this point we've covered two scenarios of when to sell because of 1) big gains or 2) big losses. But here's the thing. A more likely scenario is that silver just goes along pretty steady, up a little here and down some there. And most investors will just be quietly accumulating more silver. So most of the time things could be pretty normal - even boring.

But here's another way to look at this. And that is that during this normal, boring period you are diverting a small portion of your savings into real money that holds its value over time, versus fake paper and electronic money that loses value over time. Recall our chart from Chapter 2 that illustrated this.

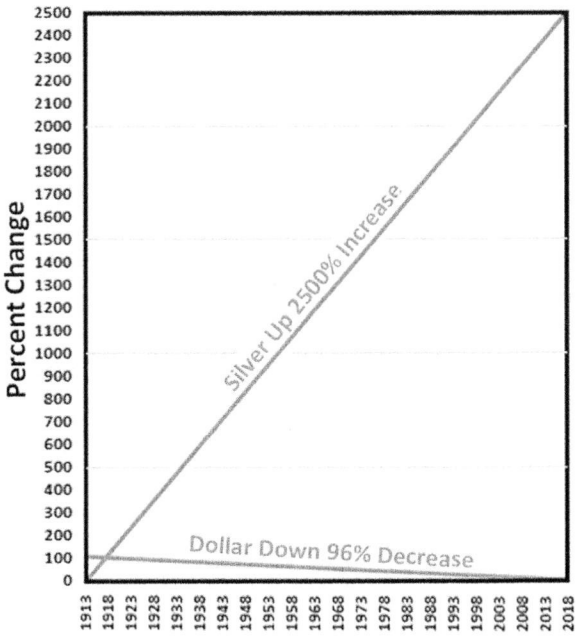

Figure 5-4. 1913 To 2018 - Dollar And Silver - Where Would You Like Your Money To Be?

And that's okay - even good. Because it means you are accumulating more silver at reasonable, or below market values. Which means you will have more to sell, and more profits to take, if and when the next silver boom hits.

Listen To The Experts

Another good way to know when to sell or stay abreast of the silver market is to listen to the experts. So for those who'd like to hear current opinions, we'll look at some of my favorite expert's publications and sites.

Now before we get into these, note that there are very few strictly silver investment newsletters out there, and most are quite pricey. There are more gold and silver investment newsletters, but they are quite pricey too.

And most beginning silver investors can't afford them and don't need them. After all, they're just starting out and steadily accumulating silver as we described earlier. So for those reasons, I've included sites with free reports and newsletters.

Now keep in mind that many of these sites will also be selling newsletters or precious metals as well. But you don't need to buy (unless you want to) to sign up for their free newsletters or read their free website articles.

Also, please note that I have no business affiliation with any of the sites or experts, aside from being a reader of many of their articles and posts.

Sprott Precious Metals Watch

The Sprott Precious Metals Watch blog is produced by Eric Sprott - a Canadian businessman, precious metals fanatic and leading expert in silver and gold. And he's put his money where his mouth is, as a self-made billionaire who has made most of his wealth in silver and gold.

The FREE blog posts numerous quality articles on precious metals every week. A large number of them are about gold, but there are plenty of articles on silver as well. Also note that the posts are a consolidation of Sprott and other expert sites.

For example, below is a sample of silver articles from the blog at writing...

- *Precious Metals and Miners Soar in 2019* by Sprott
- *Global Silver Market Forecast to Shine in 2020* by The Silver Institute
- *Exposure To Gold And Silver Via The Sprott Physical Gold And Silver Trust* by Seeking Alpha
- *Perfect Storm for Silver* by Visual Capitalist

You can access the blog for free at https://www.sprott.com/precious-metals-watch/.

If the name Sprott sounds familiar to you, that may be because he created the Sprott Physical Silver Trust (PSLV) fund we mentioned back in Chapter 4 on different types of silver investments. He also offers many other precious metals products, which you may see at the main site https://www.sprott.com.

Needless to say, I pay attention to anything he writes.

GoldSilver Blog

This free blog is published by Mike Maloney, who is a world renowned expert in the Gold and Silver market. I find the blog to be informative, with current articles and videos about gold and silver.

You can access it at www.goldsilver.com/blog. They also have a free newsletter, which I subscribe to, and you can to. Just look for GoldSilver Email News at the blog site and enter your email address.

And they also have interesting videos about gold and silver. For example, at writing was a fireside chat video about *Why Should You Have Exposure to Silver Now?* It's a discussion between Jeff Clark of GoldSilver and Keith Neumeyer, CEO of First Majestic Silver (AG) filmed at the Vancouver Resource Investment Conference.

Among other things they talked about the potential for $100 an ounce silver, as well as how some silver stocks can jump $3 a share for each $1 a share jump in silver. For silver enthusiasts, I'll bet you'll get pretty fired up as you watch and listen to CEO Keith's comments. You can see the video here https://goldsilver.com/blog/why-should-you-have-exposure-to-silver-now-keith-neumeyer-jeff-clark/.

Also note that Malony's www.GoldSilver.com site is owned and operated by Gold & Silver Inc., out of Santa Monica, CA. It's also an online dealer that sells Gold and Silver bullion which is delivered directly to your doorstep.

While I have not bought from them, at writing they show as accredited with the Better Business Bureau, and primarily sell bullion. They also sell jewelry and emergency survival food.

StreetWiseReports

This site features interviews with investing experts in the life sciences, precious metals, energy and special situations. I always click on THE GOLD REPORT tab at the top, but don't be fooled by the tab name because they also have articles on silver.

For example, at writing they had a new post on MAG Silver Corp (MAG), a mineral exploration and development company focused on the acquisition, exploration and development of projects located within the Mexican silver belt. The article discussed them moving up their production start on one of their mines in Mexico.

Sometimes they also have a stock rating with the news, and in this case it was a Buy rating with a per share price target of US$23. The stock was currently trading at around US$9.64 per share.

Besides reading their site from time to time, you can also sign up for their free resources report, The Gold Report, which is delivered by email. Just enter your email address where it says Get Our Streetwise Reports Newsletter Free. You can check out the site at https://www.streetwisereports.com/.

Casey Daily Dispatch

The Casey Daily Dispatch offers lots of free investment advice on gold, silver, stocks, bonds and real estate. Or as they say on their site, the *Casey Daily Dispatch* will point you to today's top moneymaking opportunities and prepare you for the hidden dangers in the markets.

So there will be many articles posted that are not about silver. But there's a good enough mix of silver and precious metals posts to make the site worth your while. And many of the other articles are interesting and provide a useful financial market backdrop to the investing world.

The Daily Dispatch is produced by international investor Doug Casey, who is chairman of Casey Research, LLC. Personally, I read just about anything I see that he writes. He is insightful, colorful, and fair warning here - politically incorrect. In fact, he has written a book entitled **Totally Incorrect**, which I have read and is sitting here in my library as I write.

Among other things, he is very bullish on silver and its value going up in the future. Or as he said in a recent post, "…as history shows, when gold runs, silver goes wild."

He has also written numerous other books including "Crisis Investing: Opportunities and Profits in the Coming Great Depression" (1979) and many articles for his own publications. And he's also appeared on NBC News, CNN, National Public Radio, and been featured in publications such as Time, Forbes, People, Barron's and The Washington Post.

You can see his Daily Dispatch here at https://www.caseyresearch.com/daily-dispatch/. And you can sign up for his free newsletter by entering you email address at this site (just look in the lower right of the page where it says Join Our Daily Newsletter).

SilverInstitute.org

The Silver Institute, established in 1971, is a nonprofit international association whose members span the silver industry. These include bullion suppliers, refiners, manufacturers and suppliers of silver products.

Among other things, they collect and publish statistics about consumption, production, distribution and the uses of silver and silver products.

I listed this site last because for many beginning investors, this may be way too much information. So if that's the case for you, no worries, just ignore it.

But for the real silver nerds among us, this is a definitive site and you'll want to check it out. You can visit the site at www.SilverInstitute.org.

Also, you can sign up for their free newsletter. Just enter your email at the bottom of the screen where it says SIGN UP FOR OUR NEWSLETTER.

6

HOW MUCH SILVER SHOULD YOU OWN?

Okay, so we've made the case that most people should own some silver. And that fits with most financial advisor's recommendation's that people own some precious metals in their investment portfolio. But just how much in precious metals, and silver, should you own?

Opinions vary rather widely on this, so let's look into it and narrow down the choices.

One advisor, who is very concerned about the risk to currencies right now, feels that 33% of a portfolio should be in precious metals. And he would have most of that 33% in gold (70-80%) and a smaller part of it in silver (20-30%).

So that would be around 10% of a total portfolio in silver and 23% in gold for a total of 33% in precious metals. (Note I used his high end of 30% silver of 33% precious metals =.099% rounded = 10%).

So in a $100,000 portfolio, based on his recommendation, you would have $10,000 in silver and $23,000 in gold, with the remaining $67,000 in stocks and other investments.

That feels a bit extreme to me. True, if the currency collapsed or there was a serious financial crisis, that might be a good place to be. But we can't make all of our financial decisions based on some slim possibility of disaster. After all, life tends to go on, day by day, pretty much the same.

So we want to invest accordingly, while still affording some protection against disaster and preserving our purchasing power. And also being prepared to make a good deal of money if the price of silver does rocket higher in the future.

So let's look at another opinion. This one, from a very credible expert, is based on an actual study. It showed that the best mix for conservative, average and aggressive investors to be 7.1%, 12.5% and 15.7% in precious metals. These percent's gave the best financial results for those groups of investors.

Now this study included gold, silver and platinum as the precious metals. So using silver as a third of those precious metals, we could say the silver guideline is 2.3% for conservative investors, 4.1% for average and 5.2% for aggressive investors. And since none of this is an exact science, let's just smooth those numbers out to 2%, 4% and 6% respectfully as an easy guideline.

That seems more balanced and realistic to me. And, like I said, it was based on a study to maximize investor return.

Then in another report from another very credible source, initially recommended no more than 10% in silver, but then in a later update raised that to a maximum of 25% in silver.

And yet another advisor felt that people should own more silver than gold, and recommended that 60-70% of their precious metals investments should be in silver. So using the earlier study, we could say the silver recommended to be 5% for conservative, 9% for average and 11% for aggressive investors.

And finally, in another credible portfolio allocation book, the author recommends 5% of a total portfolio be in precious metals. Assuming that's silver and gold, we could say 2.5% in silver.

Wow - so that's a pretty wide range of opinions, with 2.3% on the low end and 25% on the high end.

But all that said, I think it's best not to go too overboard with all of this. Because silver can go up and down pretty rapidly.

So while there's a good case for owning it, and anticipating it's price to soar sometime in the future, no one knows when that is. And it could go down before going up. And that could cause some pretty big swings in your portfolio if you are too heavily invested.

So to be prudent and keep it simple, I would tend to use the aforementioned study as a starting point. That is, the simple guideline of 2% silver for a conservative investor, 4% for an average investor and 6% for aggressive investors.

As of this writing I have 8% in precious metals overall (6% silver and 2% gold). And I intend to move that up over time to 10% precious metals (7% silver and 3% gold).

So I am somewhat of an aggressive precious metals investor based on the 2% conservative investor, 4% average investor, and 6% aggressive investor guideline. And that's because I do believe silver will make a big move sometime in the future, and give me some financial protection over the long run. I eat my own cooking, so to speak.

But note that I haven't gone totally crazy with this (like the 25% recommendation from one expert in the field). I keep much more of my investments in stocks than precious metals, and particularly in dividend paying stocks.

Of course, everyone's situation is different. So you'll need to decide what works best for you. But I think the 2%, 4%, 6% guideline above is a good place to start with your decision. And most people should have at least 2% of their total portfolio in silver.

And that's not too hard to do if you gradually accumulate silver over time.

7

PROTECTING YOUR SILVER INVESTMENTS

When it comes to protecting your silver investments, there are two main considerations. These are how to protect your physical silver, and how to protect your paper silver, i.e. silver stocks, funds, etc. We'll start off with your physical silver first.

Physical Silver

It's a good idea to keep some of your physical silver nearby where you can get your hands on it immediately. This is the silver you would need should some serious financial disaster occur in the economy.

Depending on your needs, this might be 50 ounces, 100 ounces, or 500 ounces or more. It's your choice and all depends on what you have and think you'll need. Just note that in a financial disaster, financial institutions could be shut down. So you may not have access to silver stored with them for days or weeks - right when you need it. So consider storing some silver in your home or nearby.

Of course you'll want to put it in a secure place. Where and how you do this is up to you and your creativity. But here are a few ideas and options to get your thought process going.

For starters, we'll look at a cheap and clever way to hide your silver in plain sight. And that is to use book safes.

Book Safes

A book safe is a hollowed out book that you can store valuables in. When it's closed and sitting on a shelf, it looks like any other book. Book safes are inexpensive and readily available to buy. And for the economy minded readers, you can even make one yourself. So if you're handy, and careful, all you need is an old book and a sharp cutting knife like a box cutter.

For example, here's a handmade book safe with a radio hidden in it. This looks like some World War II secret agent spy thing, doesn't it? But you can do the same thing and stack your silver coins and bars in it just fine.

Figure 7-1. Home Made Book Safe
Courtesy www.wikipedia.com

Or you can buy premade book safes rather cheaply. Here's one listed on Amazon for under $9 - and it has a lock and key. The inside storage area measures: 6.6 x 3.3 x 1.57 inches inside a book that is 7.2 x 4.6 x 1.9 inches.

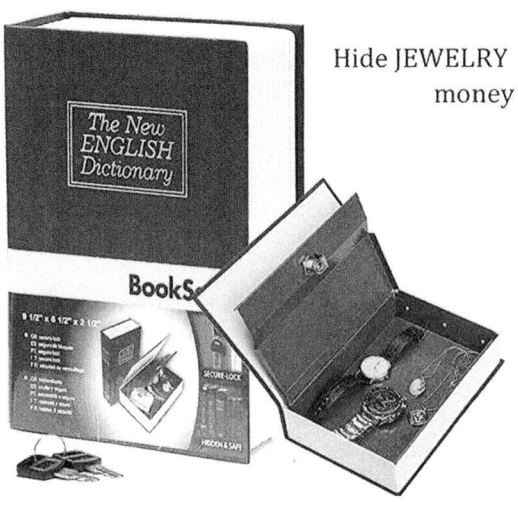

Figure 7-2. Economical Book Safe With Lock And Key

This one book safe would hold over 100 Silver eagles inside it.   So at $20 an ounce, you would be hiding over $2000 of silver - in plain sight.   And yes, I did try this - it held 104 Eagles to be exact.   Of course, silver isn't light, so, completely full, this would make for some heavy reading at about 6.5 pounds (104 ounces / 16 oz per pound).

I found this book safe by going to www.amazon.com and searching for "book safes."   Or if you want to save some money, search for "book safes under $10." All said, I don't think you have to get real expensive with this.

Of course, you'll want to buy book safes with different covers and spread them around.   Otherwise, it would look kind of conspicuous if you had five identical dictionaries sitting side by side on a bookshelf.

Now, an advantage, and drawback, to book safes is that they are portable.   So if someone knows where they are, they can just pick them up and carry them out of your house.   But typically, a burglar is not going to be thinking about your literary tastes, so book safes do offer some protection.

However, all that said, if you want more security, and less portability, then you could store your silver in a more traditional safe.

Traditional Safes

Figure 7-3. SentrySafe SFW123ES

It has a combination lock, is fire resistant and waterproof and costs $129. And it has a 1.23 cubic foot interior (12.6 in. W x 11.9 in. D x 13.8 in. H) and weighs 86 pounds.

So it's probably not something a burglar would just throw under their arm and walk out of you house with - although I guess that could happen. And speaking of weight, Walmart advertises free delivery, which sounds pretty convenient.

Another advantage to buying a safe is that it can serve a dual purpose. No doubt you have other valuables, or important papers, that need fire or theft protection. So this might justify your cost and buying decision.

And finally, as mentioned earlier, you want to keep your safe out of sight. And it's also good to secure it to the floor or wall, depending on where you locate it.

So if something like the safe above interests you, I found it by doing a Google search for "Walmart Safes." Similarly, Amazon has a wide variety of safes ranging from $25 to $225. You can find these by going to www.Amazon.com and searching for "safes." Also Home Depot has a wide variety of safes at www.homedepot.com. But please note that I don't own any of these safes. I'm just giving you a starting point in case you are interested in the idea.

And you can get even more creative with safes, so here's another idea for the truly safety conscious, and that is to have two safes.

Two Safes

This plays on the idea that once a burglar has found some valuables in your house, they will take them and leave. So you make it a bit easier to find some of your valuables.

You do this by having two safes. You can secure most of your silver in a good safe, secure and hidden away as we just described. Then you can get a cheap safe and put it in an easier to find location. Then you store a smaller amount of silver, and cash, etc. in a second, decoy safe.

This way, if your house is broken into, the burglar may find the decoy safe. And they may even be able to lug it out the door. Or, if they can open it, they may be satisfied they've found your silver and other valuables. So they take that and go, leaving your real valuables hidden away in the big safe. And of course, that was the purpose of the decoy safe after all, wasn't it.

So those are some ideas on how to keep your physical silver safe at home. But what if you want more secure, professional storage.

Safety Deposit Boxes

For more secure storage, bank safe deposit boxes come to mind. And they probably are more secure than most home storage. But before you decide to use a bank box, just be aware of some of the drawbacks.

The first of these is accessibility. After all, your bank isn't always open, so you can't access your box during those times. And that's under normal conditions. But what about crisis conditions? Because that might make accessibility even worse.

For example, on September 11, 2001, when the terrorists attacked, silver quickly rose 11%. Okay, good so far, that's what it's supposed to do in times of crisis.

But if you had your silver in a safe deposit box, you couldn't access it. Because during the week of 9/11, the banks and the stock market were closed. So no access to your silver - just when you might need it! Fortunately most people didn't so no harm, no foul that time.

But banks are starting to get pretty weird these days. In certain circumstances, they can confiscate the contents of your safety deposit box, or even move it to another location. And as they become more aligned with the federal government, those rules can get even more stringent, and change on a dime. After all, remember that President Roosevelt closed the banks to stop a bank run back in the 1930's.

And to give you a recent example of this unholy alliance, I recently went to deposit some cash in a bank account of a major US bank. Now I'm talking just a few hundred dollars, here, not thousands or anything crazy. And my reason to use cash was quite innocent - to avoid the check clearing delay so the funds were immediately available. And I had done this a few times in the past without a problem.

But this time the bank refused to accept the cash deposit. I had to go back home and get a check to make the deposit. Imagine that. A bank that wouldn't accept a cash deposit - under normal circumstances. So you can imagine how unhelpful they might be in a crisis.

So banks and safe deposit boxes do have some drawbacks. On the other hand, they provide many locations to choose from and are easy to find and use. So they are a handy option.

But if you're uneasy with their drawbacks, you might use another type of vault storage. So let's look at a simple way to do that.

Private Vault Storage Where You Buy

Another secure way to store silver is to keep it in private vaults. For example, you'll recall that I mentioned buying online from www.OWNx.com in an earlier chapter.

Well, OWNx can also store the silver for you if you don't take delivery. And their storage fees are quite reasonable. They charge a small monthly fee of 0.05% (that's five hundredths of one percent) of the value of your holdings.

And to make it easy for you, they simply deduct it from your silver holdings automatically on the first of each month. For example, if you have 20 ounces of silver in your account, 1/100th of an ounce of silver is deducted from your account to cover the storage fee.

They say your metal is safely stored at world-class, non-bank depositories. And the holdings are fully allocated and 100% insured by an all-risk policy underwritten by the world's leading specialty insurance provider.

So your holdings are completely yours; 100% ownership. This means that they are not on the balance sheet of OWNx, the depository or any other entity. And not a single ounce is used as collateral or pledged to anyone in any way.

And should you choose, you can take delivery from OWNx at any time, once you've accumulated at least 20 ounces of silver or 1 ounce of gold. But with benefits like cheap storage and their automatic purchase program, I just leave most of my precious metals in their vault for safe storage.

So those are thoughts on protecting your physical silver. But how do you protect your paper silver, i.e. your silver related stocks and ETF's and other funds. To learn more, read on.

Stocks And Funds

Aside from physical silver, your other silver investments can be in stocks and funds as we discussed earlier. Note that we'll just refer to all of these as stocks from now on to keep it simple (instead of stocks, funds, ETF's, etc.). In any event, you own these in your stock market account and you'll want to protect them too.

Because sometimes they go up in value, and sometimes they go down, just like any other investment. Now when they go up, we're happy and there's nothing in particular we need to do (unless we're speculating and want to take some profits by selling).

But when they go down we want to protect ourselves by stopping our losses before they become too great to recover from. And this is particularly important with silver stocks because the price can be so volatile. So we use protective techniques called "stop losses" like we do with any other stock or fund that we own.

When To Sell - Stop Losses

We're going to look at two techniques to control, or stop, our losses. One of them is quite simple, and will protect you from a major loss. The other is a little more involved, but believe it or not, can sometimes **get you out of a falling stock position at a profit.**

These techniques are important since most investments involve risk. And that certainly applies to silver stock investments. Because there's always the chance that once you've bought a stock, the price begins going down, and you start l   o   s   i   n   g   m   o   n   e   y   .

Now, virtually all investors lose money from time to time. But the successful investors make more money than they lose. So when a stock trade starts going down, successful investors know how to stop their losses before they get out of hand. In other words, they know when to bail out and stop their loss by selling a losing stock.
So here are two of these stop loss techniques. I use them both to control my risk, and they can help you too.

So what are we really doing when we set a stop loss? Well, we're actually deciding up front, when we buy a stock, just how much we're willing to lose before we throw in the towel and sell it. Of course we hope the stock will go up, and that often happens. But since none of us can predict the future, we have to face the possibility that the stock we are buying could go down.

And making this decision up front is the best time to do this. That's because you have no money on the table yet, so you're more objective. Let me say that another way. When you've bought a stock, i.e. you have money on the table, it's emotional. So the idea here is to get the emotions out of the process before buying the stock in the first place.

Simple Stop Loss

So here's the first technique, and that is to use a **simple 25% stop loss**. What this means is if you buy a stock, and the price goes down 25% from you purchase price, you sell it.

I call this a simple technique because many online stock accounts actually show you your percent loss or gain on the positions screen. So if you see your stock showing a -25% or worse loss, you know to sell it.

Or you can use this shortcut to calculate the stop loss stock price by just multiplying your purchase price by .75. For example, if you bought a stock for $10 a share, your stop loss price would be $7.50 ($10 X .75 = $7.50). So in this case you would sell if the stock price dropped below $7.50.

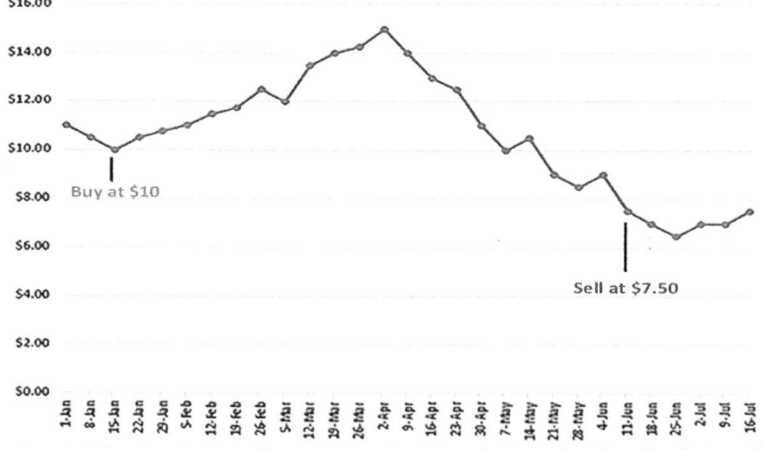

Figure 7-4. Simple Stop Loss Chart

So let's just go with that as an example. Let's say you invested in a fictional silver mining company called Lucky Silver Mining Company (LSM). Looking at our chart, let's say you bought 100 shares of LSM stock at $10 a share on January 15. So you've invested $1000. And if the stock goes down to $7.50 a share, like it did on June 18, you sell it. You've lost $250 and thrown in the towel. But you've also preserved $750 of your investment money and lived to invest another day.

Okay, so you hate losing the $250. But that's far better than having no exit plan and possibly riding the stock on down and losing even more money - which is what many beginning investors do. They turn a small problem into a bigger problem.

And here's another thing to consider. Looking at our chart again, we see that the LSM stock started turning back up after you sold it. So you might be tempted to hindsight yourself and regret that you sold it.

But don't do that. Because at the time you sold, you had no idea it was going to go back up. And it could have kept going down for a bigger loss. So best to cut your losses and bail out at the 25% loss. And by just doing this simple 25% stop loss technique, it puts you ahead of the average investor. So that's the simple stop loss technique for you.

Trailing Stop Loss

But looking at our chart, we see that after you bought LSM stock at $10 a share, it went all the way up to $15 a share. Wow - that was a pretty nice 50% profit you had going on there.

Hmmm... but the simple 25% Stop Loss rule means you rode it all the way down from $15 a share to $7.50 a share. That seems kind of inefficient, doesn't it?

Figure 7-5. Trailing Stop Loss Chart

So here's a thought. What if we calculate our 25% from the highest price it's ever been since we've owned the stock - instead of calculating with our purchase price. For example, on Jan 15 when we bought it at $10, the stop loss amount would be $7.50 like in our earlier case. But skipping across the chart to Mar 5, we see the stock has gone up to $12 a share. So now our stop loss, the price we would sell at, would be $9 ($12 X .75 = $9).

In other words, we follow, or trail, the price of the stock if it's going up, and use that new higher price to calculate our new stop loss. And we never reduce that new stop loss amount. It can only go up or stay the same. And this technique is called a **trailing 25% stop loss.**

So if the stock dropped to $9 after Mar 5, then we would sell, instead of waiting for it to go all the way on down to $7.50. Hey, that's better already, because getting out at that point would only lose $100 instead of $250.

Now skipping across the chart again to Apr 2, we see the stock has gone all the way up to $15 a share. So our stop loss price trails the stock price up even more. And with the stock price at $15 a share, our new stop loss amount is now $11.25 ($15 X .75). So if the stock price in the future drops below $11.25, we would sell the stock.

Wow - that's better yet. Because that means that even if our stock starts losing and going down from that point, we get out at a profit. We bought at $10 a share and sold at $11.25 a share for a nice 12.5% profit of $125. That's a pretty nice turn of events for a stock that started going down precipitously after April 2, wouldn't you say.

So that's the advantage of trailing stop losses. They can reduce the amount you lose. And sometimes, you even get out of a losing stock AT A PROFIT. Nice.

Now the disadvantage to this technique is that it's a little trickier to do. You have to keep recalculating and evaluating what your new stop loss is every time your stock goes higher - up to the highest point since you owned it.

Contrast that to the simple 25% stop loss technique where you just calculated your stop loss once in the beginning based on your purchase price. And like we said earlier, most stock accounts actually show you your percent loss anyhow. So you can just look at the screen and see any time that it shows -25% or worse then you need to sell. No calculation is required on your part.

Which One Should You Use?

So which technique should you use?

Well, the decision is yours. So ask yourself which one will you realistically do? Because consistently doing a simple technique is better than inconsistently doing a more sophisticated technique.

And here's another consideration for you. I mentioned earlier that I use both techniques depending on the stock. So here's how I decide. When I'm buying a stock as a speculation, I use the **trailing 25% stop loss**. By speculating, I mean the main reason I bought the stock is I think it will go up in value, and I'm looking to profit off of that. So the trailing technique gives me a better chance to sell at a profit.

But another reason I invest in silver is for protection; to preserve value against inflation, and to have some protection in case there is a financial crisis. So for that reason I typically use the simple stop loss technique. And in fact, instead of 25%, I often make my stop wider to 33%. That's because silver prices can move up and down a lot, and I want to hang on to my silver investment as long as possible for that protection.

And here's another reason I use the simple 33% stop loss. And that's because I am "investing," in a number of silver stocks because they pay me to own them by sending me cash dividends.

So I really want to hang on to these if I can. Because they are paying me to invest in them, and they are protecting me from inflation or a financial crisis, and they may also go up like if I was speculating. That's a pretty good situation all around if you ask me.

For example, I currently own a position in a stock called Wheaton Precious Metals. They are a silver streamer we mentioned earlier in the book. And they pay a dividend. Based on my purchase price of $17.83 per share, they are paying me a 2% dividend.

That's pretty impressive since the biggest complaint against precious metals investments is they don't pay you anything. And compare that to this fact. The average dividend paid by the top 500 stocks in the US stock market in Aug, 2019 is 1.92%. So I'm getting paid more than that average.

So that dividend is paying me $36 per year for every 100 shares I own, or about $3 a month. Okay, that's not big money, but it's free. And I get all the other benefits of silver as well. And so I want to hang on to those stocks unless the market just really turns against me.

But if this stock dropped to a loss of 33%, would I care? Yes - most definitely. As much as I would want to keep them, I'd bail out and sell. Because at that point I want to control my risk and stop any further losses.

So that's how I use both stop loss techniques. I typically use the trailing stop loss for speculative stocks, and the simple stop loss for dividend paying stocks. That's my preference.

Of course you can use the trailing stop loss on dividend stocks as well, and some advisors suggest that. Or you can use the simple stop loss on all of your stocks. And you can use 25% instead of the wider 33% I use just for silver related stocks. It all depends on your personal circumstances. And what you think you'll really execute consistently.

Because like we said, a simple, less efficient method, executed well is still better than a more involved but efficient method executed poorly. So both of these tools are available to you, and the choice is yours.

But however you chose, be sure to use a stop loss to control your risk with your paper silver, i.e. your silver related stocks, ETF's and funds.

8

CONCLUSION

You've gained a lot of valuable information at this point. You've seen how our paper and electronic currency is going broke. But that silver, the ultimate form of money, preserves its value over time. And remember, this is not just theory.

You recall our gasoline story we started the book with, right? How one silver quarter could buy a gallon of gasoline in the 1960's, and can still buy a gallon of gasoline today!

And now you have that insight and much more. So congratulations on completing the book, because there are very few people that understand the importance of owning precious metals like silver.

To recap, you've learned...

- How the price of silver could explode in the future.
- How silver is undervalued today by the general public.
- How buying now could increase and preserve your wealth over time.
- How silver could help protect you in a financial crisis.
- How to find and buy your first silver bullion.
- The best silver coins to invest in when you start.
- And even how you can open an automated silver buying account.
- And for those who want to take it to another level...
- ...how to invest in silver related stocks and funds.
- And how to protect your silver investments.

Now it's up to you to use this information to start building and preserving your future wealth with silver.

Don't waste time and regret thinking you should have done this a long time ago. Just remind yourself of the old adage that says, "The best time to plant a tree is 20 years ago; the second best time is now."

There's no time like the present.

So I want you to immediately apply what you've learned. Don't just close this book and move on to something else. Instead, look up a local coin dealer or online dealer. Then check them out and buy your first real, physical silver bullion. This can be in the form of American Silver Eagles, Canadian Silver Maple Leafs, or other physical silver choices we discussed.

Now you're on your way. Then just keep building your silver stack with regular or automated purchases. Rinse and repeat. And over time, your silver investment will grow.

The point here is to just get started and preserve part of your wealth the way the wealthy do. Because there's a good probability that the best lies ahead for silver. And that someday, the silver price will likely rocket upward again.

So high in fact, that people will form long lines to cash in their silver at local coin and pawn shops. And ladies will be selling their tea sets, families hocking their silverware and coin collectors cashing in their collections.

And you'll be ready, ahead of the crowd, having secured a better financial future for you and your family with silver.

Welcome to the club, and wishing you the best as a new silver investor!

John

http://www.LiveLearnAndProsper.com

Additional Resources

At this point, you've learned all the basics you need to start investing in silver. I've given you the exact steps to use to get started. Essentially, these are the same steps I have come to use over the years. I say "essentially," because my path was not so simple and direct. And that's because I didn't have a book like this years ago when I got started.

But you now have the same basic system I would use to get started today. With that said, we covered a lot of resources in the book. So this section lists them all for you as a handy reference. And there are some additional handy resources listed for you as well.

NOTE that print book readers can access this chapter and the live links at www.LiveLearnAndProsper.com/si.

Live, Learn And Prosper
www.LiveLearnAndProsper.com
Our parent website with numerous articles on silver investing, and general stock investing as well. You can also sign up for the free newsletter which comes out every month or so here at www.LiveLearnAndProsper.com/siln.

Silver Price And Charts
www.silverprice.org
This handy site gives you the current silver price, recent charts and historical charts. It also shows the gold price and Bitcoin price.

Gold Silver Blog
www.goldsilver.com/blog
This free blog offers numerous videos and current articles about silver and gold. They also have a free newsletter which you can subscribe to. Just look for where it says GoldSilver Email News on the blog site and enter your email address.

The Casey Daily Dispatch
https://www.caseyresearch.com/daily-dispatch/
Offers lots of free investment advice on gold, silver, stocks, bonds and real estate. And you can sign up for the free newsletter by entering you email address at this site (just look in the lower right of the page where it says Join Our Daily Newsletter).

Sprott Precious Metals Watch Blog
https://www.sprott.com/precious-metals-watch/
This blog posts numerous quality articles on precious metals every week. A large number of them are about gold, but there are plenty of articles on silver as well.

The Gold Report
https://www.streetwisereports.com/
This is part of the Streetwise Reports Newsletter. You can access it on the site by clicking The Gold Report tab at the top of the screen. The report contains precious metals articles including silver. Besides reading their site from time to time, you can also sign up for their free resources report, The Gold Report, which is delivered by email. Just enter your email address where it says Get Our Streetwise Reports Newsletter Free.

OWNx - Buy Physical Silver Online With Optional Automatic Purchase / Storage
http://www.OWNx.com/
OWNx.com is a precious metals custodial dealer based in Lawrence, Kansas in the US. They are my favorite online dealer because of their automatic purchase program. Another feature of OWNx that I like is that you can store your precious metals in OWNx's vault - hence the term "custodial dealer." And their premium and storage fees are quite reasonable, so that's what I do. I let them worry about keeping my silver safe. Or you can take delivery once you've accumulated at least 20 ounces of silver or 1 ounce of gold.

JM Bullion - Buy Physical Silver Online Delivered To Your Door
http://www.jmbullion.com/
JM Bullion, a precious metals products retailer, provides a convenient, straight forward way to buy your silver online. Established in 2011, they are located in Dallas, Texas in the US. They deal exclusively in physical bullion, selling silver (and gold, platinum,, etc.) that is delivered directly to your door.

Book Safes
Amazon has a nice assortment of book safes you can view here at https://www.amazon.com/s?k=book+safes&ref=nb_sb_noss_1. Or if you're reading a paper copy of this book, just go to www.amazon.com and search for "book safes." If you want to save some money, search for "book safes under $10." All said, I don't think you have to get real expensive with these.

Silver ETF Channel
https://www.etf.com/channels/silver-etfs
Lists 13 silver Exchange Traded Funds (ETF's), with ratings and holdings.

The Silver Institute
http://www.silverinstitute.org
A great resource for those interested in all kinds of statistics on supply and demand at the Silver Institute Site. They also have a free publication called the Silver News. Just look under their News and Events section to review and sign up.

List Of Countries By Silver Production
https://en.wikipedia.org/wiki/List_of_countries_by_silver_production

Silver Stock Dividend History
http://www.dividendchannel.com/
Shows the history of dividend payments that have been made for a stock, including silver stocks, funds and ETF's. The history can go back ten years and more. Like most sites, just enter the stock symbol at the top and click search. This is an excellent site and I use it frequently.

US Debt Clock
http://www.usdebtclock.org/
You can see how fast the US debt is rising in real time, second by second, by looking at this site. The numbers in the amount fields just fly by as you watch it. It's truly alarming. For example, in the minute I took to write this small factoid, the national debt went up $2,300,000 dollars. All of this debt will be covered by printing paper or electronic dollars. It makes you want to go out and buy silver coins, i.e. real money.

Free Stock Information and Charts
https://finance.yahoo.com/
Very useful to research a specific silver stock, or any stock in general. Just enter the stock symbol at the top of the screen and click the Search Finance button. You will find a wealth of information, including the dividend amount and yield. The site also has good charts of the historical stock prices. You can also get to this site by going to www.Yahoo.com and then clicking the Finance tab.

Tracking Your Stop Losses
https://tradestops.com/
Very useful if you have many different stock positions and want to use sophisticated stop loss tracking. I subscribe to it, but it is a paid for subscription service. And it's not necessary for beginners with just a few stock positions. You can use your discount brokers free alert system instead.

Discount Broker Web Sites
For those interested in trading silver related stocks and funds, you will need to have a stock market account with a broker. If you don't have an account, here's a list of discount brokers you could set one up with.
1. TDAmeritrade - www.tdameritrade.com
2. E*Trade - www.etrade.com
3. Fidelity Investments - www.fidelity.com
4. Charles Schwab - www.schwab.com
I've used TDAmeritrade for years.

BOOK: When The ATM's Go Dark by Jaclyn Frakes (Author) and Bonner & Partners (Author)
An interesting book on how to survive the end of America's 30 Year Credit Boom. This is not really a prepper or end of world book. Rather, it goes into how fragile our credit based economy is, what a credit collapse might look like, and surviving in the age of dying credit. Hint: Owning some precious metals like silver and gold are part of this plan.

BOOK: The Creature from Jekyll Island: A Second Look at the Federal Reserve by G. Edward Griffin
A fascinating book on the Federal Reserve, and their grand illusion called money. For example… where does money come from, where does it go, who makes it, the cause of wars, boom-bust cycles, inflation, depression and prosperity.
This is not a light read (600 pages) but very interesting and relevant to the need for silver investing. It changed my world view of banking and money a couple of decades ago, and could change your world view too.

VIDEO - Why Should You Have Exposure to Silver Now?
Interesting fireside chat video between Jeff Clark of GoldSilver and Keith Neumeyer, CEO of First Majestic Silver (AG) filmed at the Vancouver Resource Investment Conference. Among other things they talked about the

potential for $100 an ounce silver, as well as how some silver stocks can jump $3 a share for each $1 a share jump in silver. For silver enthusiasts, I'll bet you'll get pretty fired up as you watch and listen to CEO Keith's comments. You can see the video here https://goldsilver.com/blog/why-should-you-have-exposure-to-silver-now-keith-neumeyer-jeff-clark/.

More Books By John

Stock Investing For Beginners - How To Buy Your First Stock And Grow Your Money

The upper ten percent use stocks to grow their income and wealth. Here's just what you need to get started and join the club. You will be able to buy your first stock by the end of this book. Available in eBook and print format.

Your Future Paychecks And Raises - Get Dividend Checks In Your Mailbox Paid To The Order Of YOU!

Investing in dividend stocks is one of the most profitable ways to invest. That's because YOU GET PAID while you invest. They will actually send you checks in the mail. And you don't have to wait a long time, either. You can get your first check in 30 - 90 days. Learn how to get these checks, and how they allow you to build your future paychecks and raises too. You will learn where to find these profitable stocks, how to invest in them, and start getting your first checks – PAID TO THE ORDER OF YOU. Available in eBook and print format.

Silver Investing For Beginners - Invest In REAL Money Today For A Wealthier Future Tomorrow

The dollar has lost over 40% of its value in the last ten years. But silver has served as honest money for mankind for thousands of years. Learn how investing in silver today can increase your future wealth while the dollar continues to drop. And you can invest for just $3 to begin. Even a child can use the $3 technique - and some do. Available in eBook and print format.

Stock Market For Beginners - Simple Steps To Get Started And Achieve Your Goals

If you liked *Stock Investing For Beginners*, this is a large, easy to read paperback with additional chapters covering many more useful topics. Similar to *Stock Investing For Beginners*, it covers how most wealthy people are business owners. And it reveals how stocks are the easiest way for you to become a business owner and increase your wealth. By the end of the book you will be able to buy your first stock. Available in print format.

Thank You

Before you go I'd like to say "thank you" for purchasing my book.

I know you could have picked from hundreds of books, but you took a chance with my book.

So a big thank you for buying it and reading it all the way to the end.

If you liked this book, then I could use your help. Could you please take a moment to leave a review of this book on Amazon.

Your important opinion and feedback will help me continue to write the type of books that help you get results. And if you really liked it, please let me know at JohnRoberts@LiveLearnAndProsper.com.

ABOUT THE AUTHOR

JOHN ROBERTS is the Founder and CEO of Live Learn And Prosper.com, a newsletter and website focused on getting the most out of investments and life. His books and articles are known for their easy to understand writing style explaining complex things.

He's been a life-long investor and was a former licensed Stockbroker, Financial Consultant and Senior Business Analyst. Prior to that, he managed the Corporate IT Department of a Fortune 100 Corporation. And yet earlier, served as the Senior Programmer/Designer for May Department Stores International, spending time in London, England designing and programming a large scale international foreign buying system. He also served in the United States Marine Corps.

But all is not work and investments in John's life. Called a renaissance man by his friends, he is also an award winning photographer, cartoonist, published author and avid sailor, believing that life should be an adventure.

He recalls one Thanksgiving finding himself singlehandedly sailing his boat the *Saline Solution* in the Florida Keys — on the far edge of tropical storm Keith. He says when he finally made it back safely to port, it was the most thankful Thanksgiving of his life. He also allows this may have been a bit too much adventure.

John's had a life-long commitment to self-improvement and achieving goals. He had an early start with higher goals as a "lettered" fiberglass pole-vaulter in high school, clearing 12' when the world record was 17'.

John currently resides in Orlando. Florida. When he's not busy writing you can often find him sailing or soaking up sun at the beach.

Printed in Great Britain
by Amazon

19859177R00089